Top Talent Sourcing Tools for Recruiters

By: Jonathan Kidder

"The world of talent sourcing has been waiting for a book like this - expert, independent review of some of the most popular and useful sourcing tools in the market. Pretty certain there isn't another book like it. If you're spending money on buying sourcing tech this year, you need to buy this book." --Hung Lee, Recruiting Brainfood Curator

"Navigating the chaos of the recruiting and research technology landscape takes time and dedication. Jonathan has organized and consolidated his expertise rather than cultivating every available option. Highly recommended reading." --Aaron Lintz, Senior Talent Sourcing Specialist

"I have found this book to be a great resource for every level of Recruiter. The function and highlights are explained very well. This resource should be a staple in any Recruiters toolbox." ---Michael Crouse, Senior Global Talent Acquisition Manager

"Half the battle of finding qualified candidates is knowing what is available to utilize and so many recruiters aren't cognizant of the magnitude of resources in existence. This book provides a solid foundation for any talent acquisition professional to gain awareness of tools and methods essential for modern sourcing." --Erin Mathew, Talent Sourcing Manager

"Jonathan Kidder is easily among the top 10 Talent Sourcers in the United States. He lives and breathes recruiting, and his constant recruiting innovations, tools, observations, and recruiting products make him a truly unique sourcing leader. 'Top Talent Sourcing Tools' is a must-read book for anyone who wants to improve their recruiting trade, and everyone from the recruiting newbie to the 30+ year veteran will learn something new. I have his book on my desktop and reference it whenever I need new sourcing ideas or what to impress an audience of hiring managers or candidates. I follow everything Jonathan says because I always learn something new." --Luke Doubler, Principal Owner of RecruiterCentral

"Sourcing tools are the evergreen question also at our organization. Which one should we use? Which are still up-to-date? Which are the best? How do we know when there are so many? Jonathan has created the ultimate sourcing stack of top tools and resources you should go through. It is going to save you a lot of time testing them out yourself. Our people at GoodCall are definitely getting this book as a homework." --Josef Kadlec, Trainer, Speaker, Author, and Founding CEO of Recruitment Academy

"If you've ever wondered what tools the top recruiters are using, wonder no longer! Jonathan Kidder has done the research for you! Want to know about the best chrome

contact-finding extensions, web scraping tools, or AI Automation tools? You have to read this book!" --Bret Feig, Talent Acquisition Lead

"I totally disagree with Jonathan, the Author of this book! The way that he describes his book as a 'beginner's guide' is incorrect. This is an incredible resource for anyone, and everyone, in the Recruitment World – regardless of whether you have been working in this industry for 6 months, 6 years, or even 16 years... The tips and tricks mentioned here are valuable resources that all Recruiters and Sourcers should take the time to read, investigate and then implement what they feel works best for them. Thanks for taking the time to consolidate all of these tools in this awesome repository – the community thanks you WizardSourcer 😊" --Vanessa Raath, Founder of The Talent Hunter

"Jonathan has his finger on the pulse of what is going on in recruitment today, a knack for seeing which tools are going to aid in identifying where the talent is. His philosophy is one that others should adopt: tools are there to help you, but no one tool can do it all. The technology is ever-changing, and Jonathan highlights the need for recruiters to be constantly learning and tinkering." --Pete Radloff, Sr. Technical Sourcing Recruiter

"A tool is only as effective as the person using it. And a toolbox is only as useful as the tools in which it contains. In this book Jonathan literally covers a multitude of tools from A-to-Z, and in doing so has created a comprehensive and easily digestible resource to help navigate the ever-changing landscape of internet research and modern-day sourcing." –Marvin Booker, Senior Recruiter

"The number of tools and the amount of technology available to sourcers is truly breathtaking, but in this book Jonathan Kidder has made it easy for you to know which ones could work best for your sourcing needs. It's one book you'll want to have sitting in easy reach so you can refer to it time and time again." --Katrina Collier, Author of The Robot-Proof Recruiter

Table of Contents

Legal Disclaimer   12

About Jonathan Kidder   15

Chapter 1: Introduction to Talent Sourcing   18
    Talent Sourcers vs Recruiters
    Why is Talent Sourcing Important?
    What Does a Sourcer Do?
    How has the Role Changed?
    Will Sourcing be around in 15-20 years?

Chapter 2: Getting Started   27
    Understanding The Difficulty Rating
    What Is A Browser Chrome Extension?

Chapter 3: Contact Finding Tools   30
    RocketReach
    Nymeria
    Loxo
    PreContactTool
    Improver
    SwordFish
    Entelo
    Hiretual (hireEZ)
    Lusha
    ContactOut
    SeekOut
    AmazingHiring
    SignalHire

SocialList
SalesQL
DeveloperDB
jobin

Chapter 4: Email Tools   68
Snov.io
Hunter
Toofr
Webdef
GetEmail
GetProspect
LeadIQ
Leadleaper
Skrapp
Whoknows
Anymail Finder
Discoverly

Chapter 5: Email Verification & Deliverability Tools   89
Verify-email
Findthatlead
Emaillistverify
Voilanorbert
Mail-Tester
Spam Check
Glock Apps
Mail Gun

Chapter 6: Web Scraping and Extraction Tools — 102
- Outwit
- Data Scraper
- DuxSoup
- Instant Data Scraper
- Dataminer + Recipe Creator
- WebScraper

Chapter 7: Automation Tools — 113
- MachineSourcer
- LinkedInHelper
- SourceWhale
- WebbTree
- Hireflow
- IFTTT
- Airtable
- Zapier
- Phantombuster
- Microsoft Flow
- Clay
- Workato.io
- Automate.io
- Elastic.io
- Blockspring

Chapter 8: Boolean Generators — 149
- (hireEZ) Hiretual Boolean Generator
- Recruitin.net
- BooleanAssistant

Bool

Chapter 9: CRM and ATS Tools   155
Google Sheets
Evernote
WhenX

Chapter 10: Email Automation   160
Gem
Interstellar.io
Resource.io
Lemlist
Trinsly
Mail Merge (Old School)
Mailchimp
SalesHandy

Chapter 11: Email Tracking Tools   175
Clearbit
FullContact
Streak for Gmail
BananaTag
Yesware
MailTrack
ContactMonkey
Hubspot

Chapter 12: People Search Engines   191
Pipl Pro
Zoominfo
Intelius

LinkedIn
LexisNexis Public Records
PeopleSmart
Yasni
FreshAddress
EmailSherlock
Spokeo

Chapter 13: Data / Tracking Tools — 209
Blogtrottr
ChangeTower
Dlvrit
Feedly
Indeed Resume
LinkedIn Recruiter and Sales Navigator
Spoonbill.io
Talkwater
Verisonista
VisualPing
Owler Alerts
Google Alerts

Chapter 14: Writing Tools — 231
Grammarly
Textio
Glossary Tech
Joblint
Gender Decoder
Text Analyzer

TapRecruit
TalVista
Applied
JobWriter.io

Chapter 15: Calendar Scheduling Tools — 247
Acuity
Calendly
Gigabook
Mytime
Setmore
YouCanBookMe
Vcita
10to8
Appointlet
ScheduleOnce

Chapter 16: Time Tracking Tools — 262
Marinara Extension
actiTime
Tracking Time
Elorus
Clockify

Chapter 17: Notable Mentions — 270
Extensity (Organization Extension)
Multi-Highlight Tool
Onetab
RecruiterWand
Text Expander

Chatgpt

Conclusion 285

Legal Disclaimer

The book's author was not paid by the companies to endorse any tool or website listed in this book. He freely gives his own personal advice on each software tool. He will not encounter any damages or liabilities associated with these tools or websites. Consult with legal counsel before you use any suggested tool. Please research your Country's privacy or GDPR before using any of the tools or suggested ideas in this book.

A Beginner's Guide to Over 50 Talent Sourcing Tools!

Are you new to the world of talent sourcing? Maybe you've heard about recruiting tools that can help find candidates online. Maybe you have trouble finding a candidate's email or cell number online?

This book is created as a guide for Recruiters and Talent Sourcers who want to learn more about the market's latest recruitment tools. This book covers free and licensed products. It does a good job of highlighting important areas of recruiting from finding leads and finding contact info, to automating outreach, tracking leads, and creating a personal ATS database or talent pipeline.

This book does a great job of explaining each area of focus and provides a high-level overview of why each tool is important to use when conducting research and recruiting top talent. There's a lot of news within the recruiting technology space and Jonathan has done a great job of condensing the list of tools down to a manageable level. The book highlights each tool, giving a rating level, explaining benefits, and telling you how and why it should be used in your Talent Sourcing strategy.

The author of this book has over a decade of research talent sourcing experience. Jonathan Kidder has trained Sourcers across the globe and he's an active blogger within the community. He launched his blog WizardSourcer.com in 2015 which focuses on helping others learn about the latest talent sourcing tools.

He's excited to share the latest recruitment tools on the market and, even more so, he's excited to help you on your journey of becoming a Wizard at talent sourcing.

Once this book was published in 2021, the tool suggestions were already out of date. Technology moves fast within the recruiting space. I wanted to highlight tools that have been tried and true for a while. The book will focus on core categories that Recruiters and Sourcers need to master in their daily routines. I recommend checking out my blog WizardSourcer.com to stay up to date on the latest tool trends.

Tools include: Browser Chrome Extensions, Contact Finding Tools, Webscraping, AI Automation, Boolean String Generators, People Search Engines, Email campaign tools, and much more!

About Jonathan Kidder

Jonathan Kidder, AKA the "WizardSourcer," is a top-ranked technical talent sourcing recruiter, staffing expert, and corporate trainer who assists organizations of all sizes in identifying and attracting top talent.

A wizard at harnessing the power of social networking, Boolean strings, search aggregators, deep web searching, scrapers, and other advanced technology tricks and tools. In 2015, he founded a recruiting blog called WizardSourcer, which has become one of the leading knowledge resources for recruiters online.

His mission is simple: To help Recruiters and Talent Sourcers stay updated on the latest sourcing trends within our community.

With nearly a decade of full-cycle recruiting and sourcing experience under his belt, he has worked in talent sourcing and recruiting with companies including Amazon, Vista Outdoor, CA Technologies, American Express, and many others.

Throughout his career as a sourcing leader, he has pursued continuous learning to stay current on the latest sourcing trends and to help clients across industries maximize the use of high-tech recruiting tools ranging from browser extensions to AI automation.

After earning a bachelor's in business from Bethel University in Saint Paul, Minnesota, Jonathan launched his sourcing career at Allegis Global Solutions, one of the world's largest RPO staffing companies.

At Allegis, Jonathan discovered the power of social media as a recruiting tool. This inspired him to develop and implement a proprietary employer branding EVP and recruitment marketing plan that could be used with any client to attract the world's best available talent.

A sought-after speaker and mentor, Jonathan has trained teams around the globe on best practices for sourcing and recruiting top talent. One of the industry's emerging go-to resources on recruiting expertise in the 21st century, he writes regularly on the latest recruiting trends for his own top-ranked blog at WizardSourcer in addition to being a contributing writer for AI recruiting platform hireEz, SourceCon.com, and Recruitingblogs.com.

He's the author of several recruiting books including:

- *A Guide to Diversity Talent Sourcing*
- *How to Become a Technical Recruiter*
- *The Art of the Recruiter Message*
- *Boolean String Basics for Recruiters*

- *LinkedIn Revealed [Free Download on WizardSourcer]*
- *The Candidate Experience*
- *Talent Sourced*
- *LinkedIn Networked*
- *Launch your Recruiting Career*
- *Productivity Hacks for Recruiters*
- *Webscraping Basics for Recruiters*
- *Talent Mapping*
- *Guide to Recruiting Military Veterans*
- *Hiring Manager's Survival Guide to Recruiting*

Jonathan was Awarded Most Prolific Recruiting Author in 2021 by Michael Kelemen

Reviewers have called Jonathan Kidder's writing "Practical, amazingly vast collection of sourcing knowledge that will make your Recruiter life easier." From just reading a few pages of Jonathan's books, it will be evident the author has spent many years practicing and honing his skills, distilling it down into easily digestible information that doesn't require the readers to be technical to understand. Every recruiter can benefit from his books! – Star Tribune 2021

Read more:
https://www.digitaljournal.com/pr/jonathan-kidder-top-ranked-recruiter-awarded-the-most-prolific-recruiting-author-of-2021#ixzz7qTzbZSAH

Chapter 1: Introduction to Talent Sourcing

What distinguishes a top-performing Sourcing professional from the ordinary ones? A significant factor in their success is their adaptability and proficiency in utilizing cutting-edge technologies.

People share a significant part of their lives on the Internet, including their interests, their affiliations and their occupation. The vast majority of qualified people for any open job are not applying for jobs, they don't have a posted resume on a job board, and their LinkedIn profile does not have enough information for us to know what skills they have. The average sourcer and recruiter will not go further than these paths that are trampled by everyone else. There is talent sourcing for the average, then there is talent sourcing for the high achievers who get to the next level of performance and success by using the tools within this book.

Sourcers are becoming an integral part of the job search market, as companies are looking for more specialized roles with fewer qualified applicants. Gone are the days when a company could post a role and easily find candidates that have exactly what they are looking for.

Talent Sourcers vs Recruiters

Talent Sourcers and full-cycle Recruiters are frequently mistaken for one another, but there are clear distinctions between the two. What distinguishes a Sourcer from a Recruiter?

Talent Sourcers are searching for potential candidates that have not applied to the role. According to Boolean Blackbelt, they are not necessarily "passive" because they could be actively applying to other roles, just not yours. In order to get that perfect candidate to know about the open role, a Sourcer finds them and gives them the information through a screening call.

During the phone screen, not only are Sourcers informing potential candidates about the role, but they are also checking to make sure they meet all of the qualifications. Once they are comfortable with the candidate, they then submit them to the role they are sourcing for.

Recruiters may also perform some sourcing, but that isn't the main focus of their role. They are managing hiring managers, screening candidates, scheduling interviews and are involved in the full-cycle process. Recruiters are more involved with the company they are partnering with, which gives them less time to focus on prospecting and searching for candidates. The optimal hiring strategy is to have both Talent Sourcers and Recruiters partnering together on roles.

Why is Talent Sourcing Important?

In a competitive job market, sourcing is a necessity. With a thriving job market, companies cannot rely solely on applicants finding their job postings. Many candidates are satisfied in their current positions and may not actively seek new job opportunities. However, a Talent Sourcer's role is to identify these passive candidates who may be open to new opportunities, especially if it involves a higher salary or expanded responsibilities. The Sourcer's job is to present these opportunities and spark interest in the candidate for a potential job change.

Sourcing is also essential for smaller companies who don't have a strong market presence. If people don't know who you are, they won't be applying even if they are looking for a new job. If your company is looking for roles requiring a specialized skill set, like many in the Tech industry, sourcing will also be very beneficial. It's unrealistic to think that the right candidate is going to happen upon your company's website to apply. While it could happen, it's a much better strategy to have Sourcers actively helping you.

What Does a Talent Sourcer Do?

Talent sourcing changed from just focusing on finding leads using Boolean String Searches. Sourcers will also actively search for applicants on social media sites for candidates who have updated their career backgrounds. LinkedIn is one of the biggest sites Sourcers can use to proactively make connections with candidates they want to engage.

Sourcers can act a bit like detectives when uncovering contact information for employees at companies with a similar profile. Cold calling is another tactic that is engaged to locate and start a relationship with the potential candidate. Sourcers also utilize texting to contact candidates. With so many millennials in the workforce, it is important to communicate in a way that is comfortable with the candidate to keep them interested.

In the past, once a Sourcer found a potential candidate profile, they would submit it to the company or Recruiter and be done. Now it is more common that they are actually building relationships and engaging those candidates. In the past, they may have just passed the information along; today they usually remain in contact with the candidate throughout the hiring process.

How has the role changed?

Talent Sourcing is defined as the process of identifying, searching, screening, and submitting candidates for an open job requisition. Talent Sourcing is the first step within the recruitment process which involves in-depth research on keywords, knowledge of skill sets, and analytical data. Recruiting for a niche role requires additional time and effort to attract passive talent within the field and that's why Talent Sourcing is so important.

This means prospecting, cold calling, and screening applicants over a phone call. In the early days of Talent Sourcing and online searching, this only involved lead generation and submitting contact information to recruiting teams. However, Talent Sourcing has evolved and now requires managing the process from the beginning of the recruiting funnel.

What's the Difference between Recruiting and Talent Sourcing?

Recruiting involves the full-cycle process from first gaining HR approvals, to publishing the job opening, to screening applicants, to submitting applicants, and setting first and final round interviews. Talent Sourcing is the process at the beginning of a recruiting funnel. You go out and actively find and prospect passive candidates and convince them to apply and become active in your process.

Does Talent Sourcing Require Special Skills?

Talent Sourcing has become the most challenging part of recruiting. Finding active and available talent is time-consuming and tough. You need to fully understand the role and what you are searching for. You also need to understand advanced search Boolean techniques. It will take years of practice to fully grasp talent sourcing and it requires a lot of investment upfront. Staffing companies may have junior level Recruiters solely focus on lead generation and candidate searching. But in general, Talent Sourcing requires advanced searching skills.

What is the Talent Sourcing Process?

The process begins with setting up a call with the hiring manager to have an intake meeting. From that discussion, you would start researching the competition, demographics, location intel (this is also called Talent Mapping). I wrote a book titled: Talent Mapping that will guide you through that full process.

With your research and data collected, you would then begin your search using advanced Boolean search techniques. You would also use recruiting tools that help automate mundane searching tasks. From there, you would reach out to candidates and try to connect with them over the phone. You would then set up a call and do a full phone screen. The phone screen would take on average 15-30 minutes where you would describe the role/team and then screen for basic skill requirements. From there, you would schedule a first round interview. After that point, it's common for the recruiter or client lead to take over the process.

Will Talent Sourcing be around in 15-20 years?

It's hard to predict the future at this point – but I can say that Talent Sourcing is here to stay.

For years now there has been a prediction about how AI is going to take over recruiting. So far there have been some tools that have helped recruiters be more efficient and better, but most of the tools out there so far have not lived up to the hype.

In comes, Open AI's Chat GPT-3 which I know is not going to replace any recruiters at the moment, but it's the best AI tool that has been released to the public.

I think we are just scratching the surface when it comes to AI Technology. I think these advances will only help improve our recruiting process and improve the candidate experience.

Our duties will probably change – but there will always be a need for connection and human relationships. Because of that, I think

Sourcing will still be around but may look different than where it is now. The main point is - we may have better tools, but a human touch and relationship will always be needed in the recruitment process.

Will Talent Sourcing be needed in the Future?

We may have industries that will still have a difficult time finding applicants. AI matching tools will continue to improve and assist Sourcers with finding talent online. It will become quicker to find a slate of active profiles and there will be tools that will automate outreaches completely. I could see the top of the sourcing funnel becoming fully automated with the help of tools and ATS systems. Sourcers will instead focus on building touchpoints within the hiring process to have a better person-to-person connection.

Because of the human factor, there will still need to be a human assisting with the recruiting process.

Communication is going to play a role in the process no matter regardless. We can push applicants through the process, but we will still need to have a call to walk them processes that can be overwhelming and complicated. This includes screening for technical based questions and answering questions on the culture/environment. To a certain extent, you could automate this by using video messaging or chatbots. Chatbots like Alexa or Siri could eventually be programmed to ask and answer phone screening questions, and this may come to fruition within the next decade.

Could AI Virtual Assistants replace Recruiters?

In the film, "Her" we see a glimpse of future AI technology and the human dating element. A rather lonely character yearns for human connection. He discovers a dating app that allows him to have a relationship with a computer. While this is an obscure take on the future it may not be that far off. Recruiting could be done with the help of AI and chatbots to screen and submit applicants, and with some advances in technology these interactions will feel more and more lifelike.

However, human connection on some level will always be needed for the candidate experience. Talent Sourcers will still be needed to assist applicants through the process but may play a different role when it comes to searching and outreach. I could see technology changing the recruitment industry completely. It could remove barriers and the need to do mundane search and sourcing tasks. Technology will improve the recruiting process and make our profession more relationally focused rather than searched focused.

Chapter 2: Getting Started

Finding highly respected tools within the sourcing community is no easy feat. If you ask a group of Recruiters what their favorite contact finding tools are, you will get many answers. With so many tools, tricks, and hacks out there, I felt a strong need to write a book like this one.

Recruiting tools are constantly changing and evolving, it's important that you stay updated with the most recent, effective, and efficient tools on the market. It's hard to stay updated on the latest tool out there. Our community can sometimes have the shiny tools syndrome. We joke about finding the perfect candidate (aka "Purple Squirrel") but I'd say some Sourcers act like squirrels jumping on the latest trend – myself included.

The truth is, there is no one tool that will do the job. You will need to have a tool belt of options to perform different tasks within your sourcing role.

With that said, this guide includes breakdowns of my favorite "foundational" tools that I consider must-haves in the following categories:

- Contact Finding Tools
- Email Tools
- Email Verification and Deliverability Tools
- Web Scrapers and Extraction Tools

- Automation Tools
- Boolean Generators
- ATS (Application Tracking) Tools
- Email Automation
- Email Tracking Tools
- People Search Engines
- Data Tracking Tools
- Writing Augmentation Tools
- Calendar Scheduling Tools
- Time Tracking Tools
- Productivity Tools

Within each section, I'll show you the best tools across these categories, how to use them effectively, give insider tips for success, and an overall difficulty rating level. I will also include screenshots highlighting each tools functionality.

Understanding the Rating System:

Each tool will have a rating level based on how difficult it is to use:

- **Beginner:** Easy to understand and use without prior knowledge of the tool or space.
- **Intermediate:** It will take some time to fully understand the tool.
- **Advanced**: More advanced which will require taking a demo of the tool.

What Is a Google Browser Chrome Extension?

Before we dive into the tool reviews, if you're not familiar with browser extensions or Chrome extensions specifically, allow me to offer a quick explanation so you can make the most of the tools I'm about to give you.

In the words of Google:

> *"Extensions are small software programs that customize the browsing experience. They enable users to tailor Chrome functionality and behavior to individual needs or preferences. They are built on web technologies such as HTML, JavaScript, and CSS."*

It's good to point out that extensions can work on other browsers like Microsoft Edge. This browser was first introduced in 2015, and also has extension capabilities. Edge includes integration with Cortana and has extensions hosted on the Microsoft Store.

Extensions generally serve one purpose, whether it's helping you quickly pull candidate contact information from their online profiles or aiding your productivity in some other way. You'll simply head to the Chrome store in your Chrome browser, search for the extension, and install it. **Now, let's explore all the tools you should be using.**

Chapter 3: Contact Finding Tools

These tools allow you to locate an individual's personal email, phone number, or office number through information readily available online. Many websites gather personal data and sell it to contact-finding platforms such as Hiretual (hireEZ) or SeekOut. The leading online contact data companies include ZoomInfo, Spokeo, and Pipl.

Why Do You Need Contact Finding Tools?

Tracking down a candidate's cell number can be quite a difficult task, but if you're convinced, they're going to be a good fit, it's definitely worth putting in the effort to locate their most recent contact info. Many tools might give you the contact details, but are they verified or up to date? There are many modern tools that can help you do just that.

RocketReach

Rating: Beginner
Features:
- Simple and easy to understand
- No need to visit LinkedIn directly
- Find email addresses and cell numbers
- Integrates with ATS and CRM systems

RocketReach is a web-based tool that enables you to find emails by searching a name, company, or LinkedIn profile URL. It boasts a 98% accuracy rate when it provides a contact lead with data, and has over 300,000 active user downloads on the Chrome store.

This tool is a convenient way to locate email addresses within a company's domain and search for specific individuals. You can find both personal and corporate emails with RocketReach, and the built-in search engine eliminates the need to visit LinkedIn.

RocketReach adheres to strict ethical standards and complies with the law. It extracts profile information through a combination of web crawling and data mining algorithms such as entity recognition and email prediction. There are various pricing packages to choose from: the essentials package for $49/month with 1,920 lookups per year, the pro package for $99/month with 4,500 lookups per year, and the ultimate package for $249/month with 12,000 lookups per year (as of 2022).

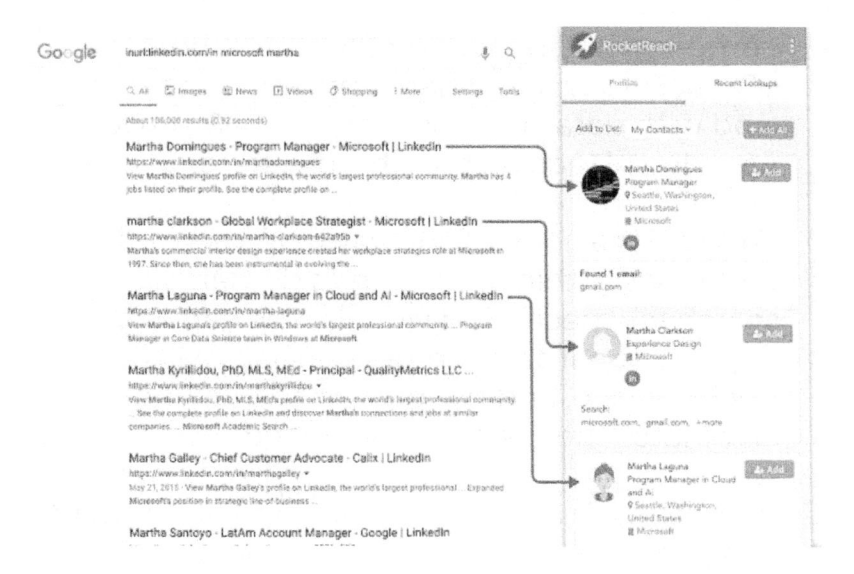

Nymeria

Rating: Beginner

Features:
- Use it while browsing LinkedIn and GitHub
- GDPR / CAN-SPAM Compliant
- Accuracy levels range from 60-70 percent on average

Nymeria is a browser extension that assists in locating email addresses on social and professional networking sites. The Nymeria extension allows you to find contact information and create lists of leads across several social media platforms, including LinkedIn, GitHub, Stack Overflow, and Dev.to. Nymeria makes the process effortless by automatically displaying emails as you browse

32

profiles on LinkedIn, providing instant access to information with just a click.

Using Nymeria, you can:

- **Find Verified Emails**: Find all emails associated with social or professional network profiles. Unlike other email finders, Nymeria only reveals verified email addresses.
- **Build Lead CSV Lists**: Create lead lists to easily categorize emails and make managing lists easier than ever before.
- **Export Leads:** Lead lists can be exported to a spreadsheet for easy sharing or processing.

Nymeria is a paid tool which offers 1000 requests for $39 per month. All packages include finding verified emails and deliverability, unlimited team members, and building your own email list.

To find emails with Nymeria, all you have to do is browse a LinkedIn or GitHub user profile; you can find the user's email address with a single click of the Nymeria badge icon in your Chrome extensions.

Loxo

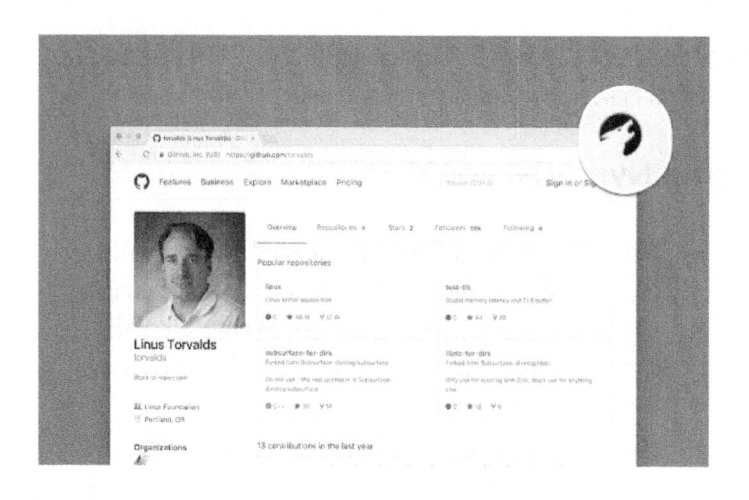

Rating: Advanced

Features:

- Uses AI automation to help you source
- Automates outreach and follow-ups
- Ranks candidates based on search criteria
- Robust applicant-tracking ATS and CRM system
- Has a contact-finding extension add-on

Loxo boasts itself as the premier Talent Intelligence Platform and a world leader in AI Recruitment Automation Software.

A standout feature is Loxo's Applicant Tracking System, which streamlines your recruitment process. This tool provides a competitive edge and enables you to hire the ideal team for your business goals.

Features include:
ATS tracking system
The applicant tracking system will help serve as the backbone to your recruiting business processes. With Loxo's automated recruiting solutions, your business will have a true hiring advantage in the emerging Web 3.0 era.

Contact Information
There are graphs and charts where big data is represented in front of the Loxo users, with over 530 million people worldwide with verified email addresses and phone numbers. The AI technology will show you similar data day by day, creating an easy database of the most compatible candidates.

AI Search Automation
Pre-build your email, SMS, phone marketing, and LinkedIn activity campaigns in advance. Set your recruitment marketing on autopilot by personalizing the sequence and number of follow-ups to maximize engagement.

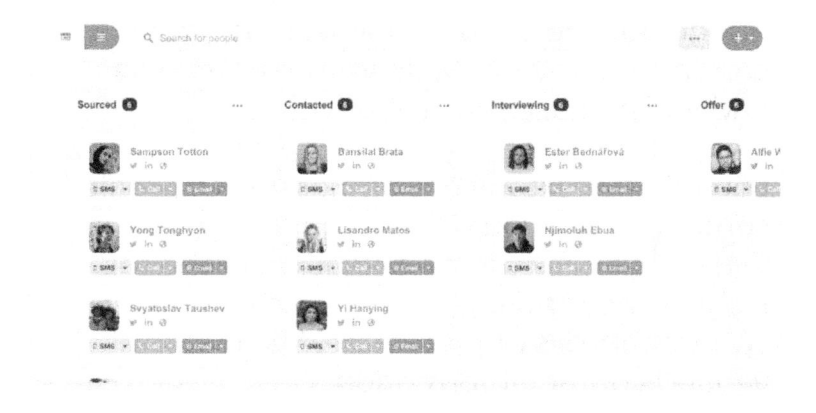

PreContactTool
Rating: Beginner
Features:
- Find verified cell phone numbers and emails
- 70-75 percent accuracy levels based on my experience
- Excellent for North American data intel

PreContactTool takes data out of the profile you are viewing to search the Internet for contact information. Use this tool to quickly find phone numbers and emails associated with the profile you're viewing. You can purchase only the amount you really need. It's roughly a dollar per contact.

Using more sources to bring information will always give you results. Phone numbers and email addresses are the focus and this tool will gather it all in a minute.

PreContactTool can deliver accuracy with greater relevance of email addresses and phone numbers found online. Plus, your credits will stay available for the entire year, and you can use them at any time.

Login in the extensions and open the profile of someone you would like to get in contact with. Then click on the extension in the top right corner and log in. Next, click on *show contact details of current profile* to see verified contact information.

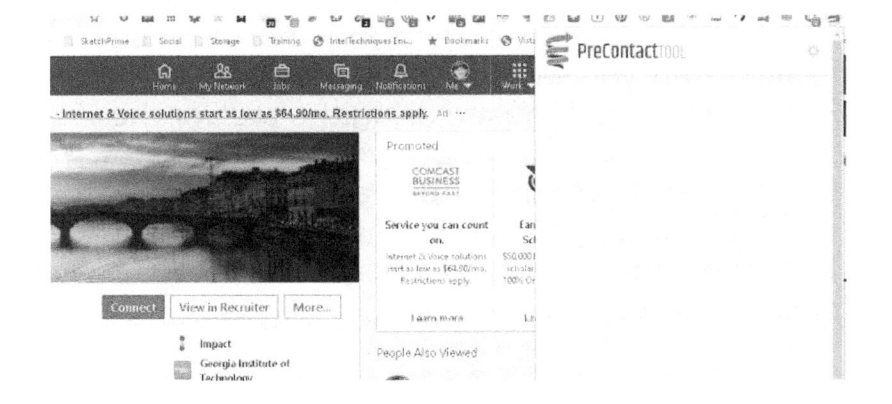

Improver

Rating: Beginner
Features:
- Works with many social media sites
- Great for collecting personal emails
- 80 percent accuracy levels overall

Improver is a Google Chrome extension for finding personal emails on LinkedIn. This tool focuses on researching emails verified on LinkedIn.

While relatively new to the world of recruiting, this tool has an 80-90 percent success rate for finding contacts for most users. It has lots of features, including a waitlist, to help you collect as much information as possible on your leads. This is an awesome tool for recruiters and talent professionals looking for vetted email addresses.

To use the Improver tool, you just need to install the Chrome extension from the official site. Then, you will need to sign up and make a new account if you are using the tool for the first time. Lastly, just open your LinkedIn profile and click the Improver icon in the upper corner of Chrome. The tool will give you a list with emails and names of the candidates.

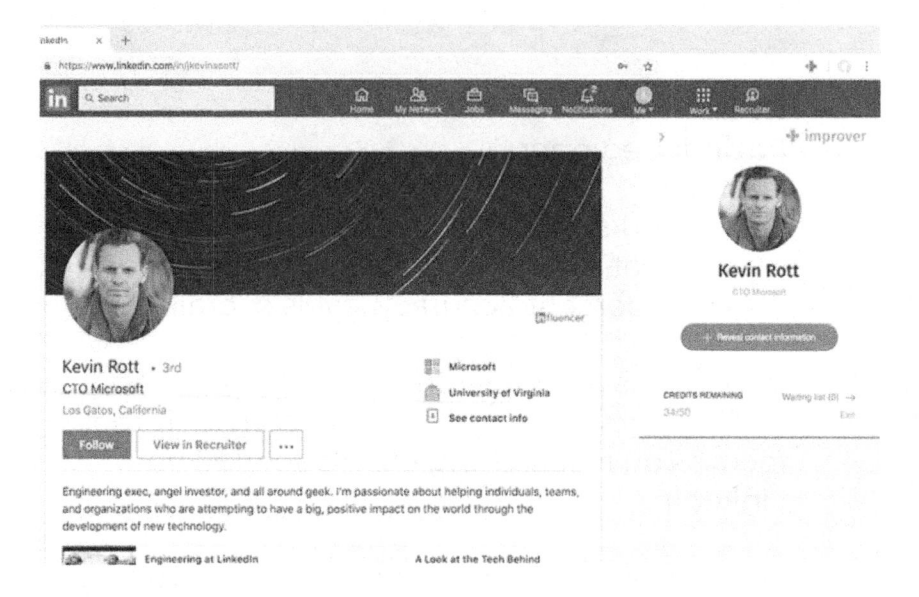

Swordfish
Rating: Beginner
Features:
- Use it with LinkedIn, Facebook, Twitter, GitHub, or Google etc.
- Locate cell phone numbers and personal email addresses
- Tools can find contact details from CSV files

38

- Accuracy levels range from 70-80 percent
- Great tool for the healthcare industry

Swordfish is an outstanding tool for recruiters seeking to obtain personal phone numbers, business contacts, and email addresses. The Chrome extension enables you to search for information from a multitude of platforms, including Facebook, LinkedIn, GitHub, Twitter, Stack Overflow, Dribble, Google, and Bing, providing extensive coverage and numerous opportunities. It guarantees access to the most up-to-date contact information.

While Swordfish is a paid tool, there is a free trial option that grants five credits, allowing you to find 25 emails or phone numbers, either personal or business.

For those just starting, the starter package offers 50 credits for $40 per month and includes the export of 100 business emails into a CSV file with your preferred data.

For $69 per month, the next package provides 100 credits for 500 business emails, along with numerous additional features.

Finally, the premier package, costing $99 per month, offers 150 credits for up to 1000 business emails.

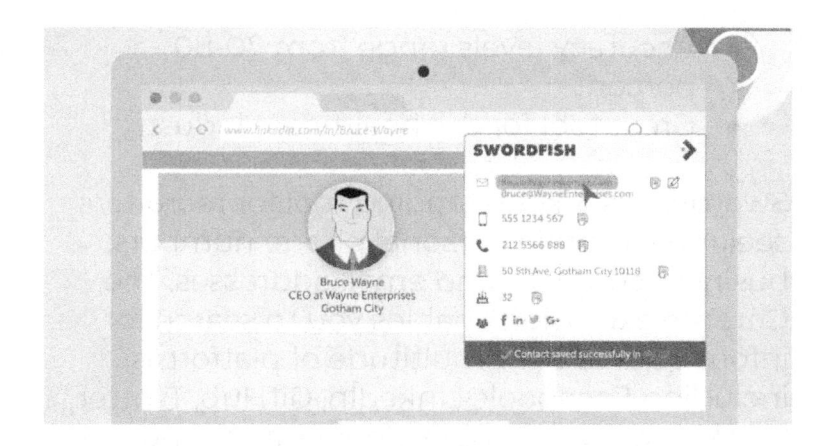

Entelo

Rating: Beginner

Features:
- AI Automation outreach software
- Email tracking
- Predictive analytics
- Diversity searching capabilities

Entelo is a cutting-edge recruitment tool that helps users find both personal and business emails online. It is designed for use by talent sourcers and professional recruiters. This cloud-based resource provides predictive analytics for the purpose of hiring and effective engagement. Entelo integrates with popular social media platforms, such as LinkedIn, Facebook, Twitter, and others.

The search engine feature enables you to locate suitable candidates for hiring, and to view their skills. Using this feature, you can gather information about potential hires, such as gender, race, age, skills, and other relevant details that can aid in the talent sourcing process.

Additionally, Entelo offers integration with Jazz, Greenhouse, and iCIMS, along with live chat support that is available 24/7. Entelo is leading the way in a new era of recruiting by utilizing predictive analytics to enhance talent sourcing automation. Other cloud-based Entelo products include an email tracking system, insights, and diversity searching tools.

Candidate Diversity Highlights
Quickly identify candidates from underrepresented groups with new candidates' badges highlighting the rich dimensions of diversity. Discover candidates who belong to groups associated with specific minorities, such as LGBTQ, Hispanic, Asian, and women's networks, as well as candidates who have championed diversity initiatives at work.

Using Entelo is a simple process. Start by creating your account. In the search bar, type in the job title or specific keyword that you want to use to search for talented individuals and hit enter. You will receive a list of potential candidates based on your keyword, including their name and surname, age, location, email, background, skills, and profession.

For example, if you search for "Web Designer", you will receive a list of web designers in a specified location with the information you selected.

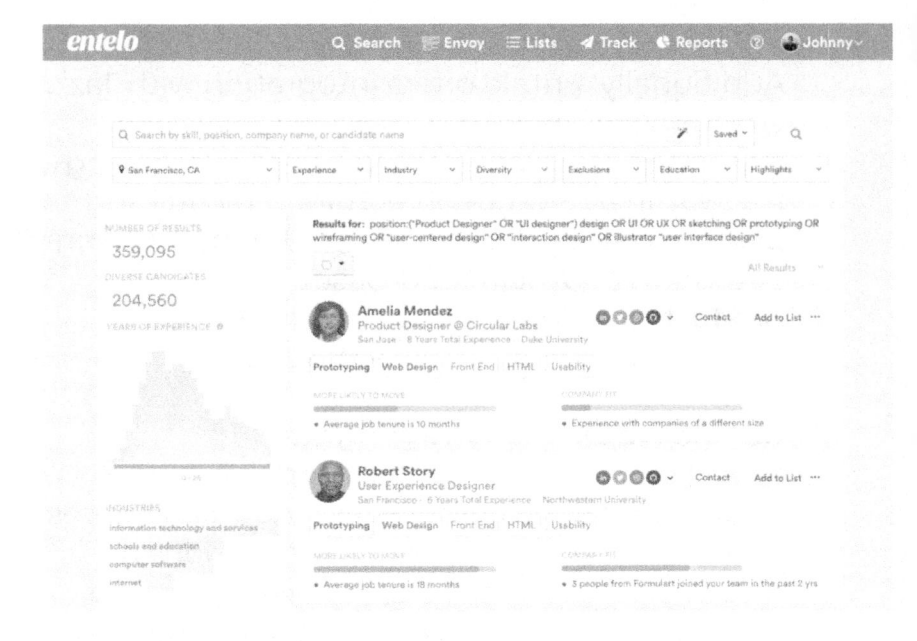

Hiretual (hireEZ)
Rating: Advanced
Features:
- Find email and cell numbers of leads
- Use AI to help you find the right people
- Tools help automate searches with AI
- Source across over 40+ platforms
- Diversity searching AI capabilities
- Email outreach with tracking

This AI-based recruiting platform vows to help you find and engage the right people 10 times faster. You can source across more than 40 platforms to quickly get the information you need and get in touch with high-quality candidates. You can source more than 750 million talents and their professional profiles across various platforms.

This tool is used for more efficient hiring across your team and increased engagement and pipeline control. You can get this tool as a Chrome extension and use it easily with just one click on the badge in the Chrome extensions field.

Hiretual is a paid Chrome extension, but you can start a free trial where you can get the contact finder and Boolean builder with three free credits per day. For $79 a month, you will get 2400 contact credits.

If you want to upgrade this package, you will get everything from this plan, plus AI sourcing, email integration on Gmail and Outlook, email templates and automation, reports, and many other features. This upgraded package is called Hiretual Essentials, priced at $169 per month.

Download Hiretual as a Chrome extension and create your profile. In the research bar, type the job name and you will get a list based on the AI-sourcing feature – candidates ready for recruiting with their contact information.

Sourcing with Hiretual's AI Search
1. Start sourcing and build an open web, AI-powered search to save to a project.

2. Calibrate the AI system by selecting either 'Good Fit' or 'Not a Fit' for the populated sample candidates, then click 'Start Sourcing.'

3. Once the search runs, decide which candidates are qualified for the role. For those that are qualified, mark as a 'Good Fit' → click the candidate's name to see more profile information.

Duplicate Checking Options
This is a great feature if you work on a large-scale team. My team has Beamery which allows us to connect and see if the applicants are already in our recruiting process. This feature is a huge time-saver.

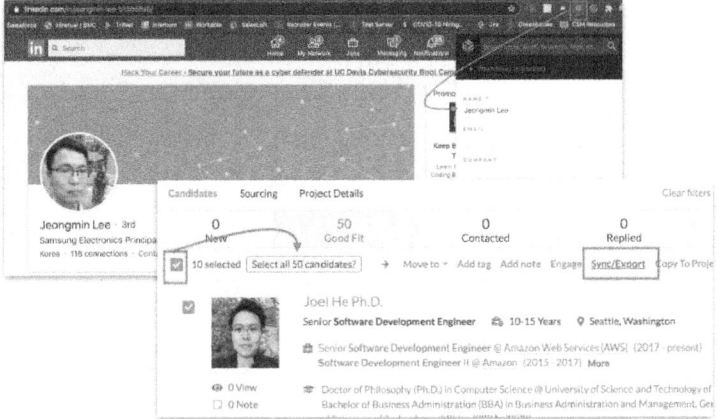

Contact Information Finding

1. Go to your preferred sourcing platform (GitHub, LinkedIn, Indeed, etc.) and source candidates. From there, choose the candidate profile.

2. Open the Hiretual Chrome extension.

3. You will see the candidate's full Hiretual profile, with direct contact information including email addresses and phone numbers.

45

4. Either add candidate to a project in the Hiretual app or click contact information to reveal it directly in the Chrome extension. You can reach out to candidates directly from there, or use your preferred method of engagement.

AI-Search Matching/Ranking
1. Navigate to your project and click into your AI-Sourcing task to begin.

2. Click 'More Filters' and apply additional filters to look at your imported list. These candidates will be ranked so that the candidates that most closely match the title and skill filters from the AI task will be at the top of the list. If you'd like to filter by experience, location, company, etc. apply relevant filters. This will filter out the candidates that don't match these criteria.

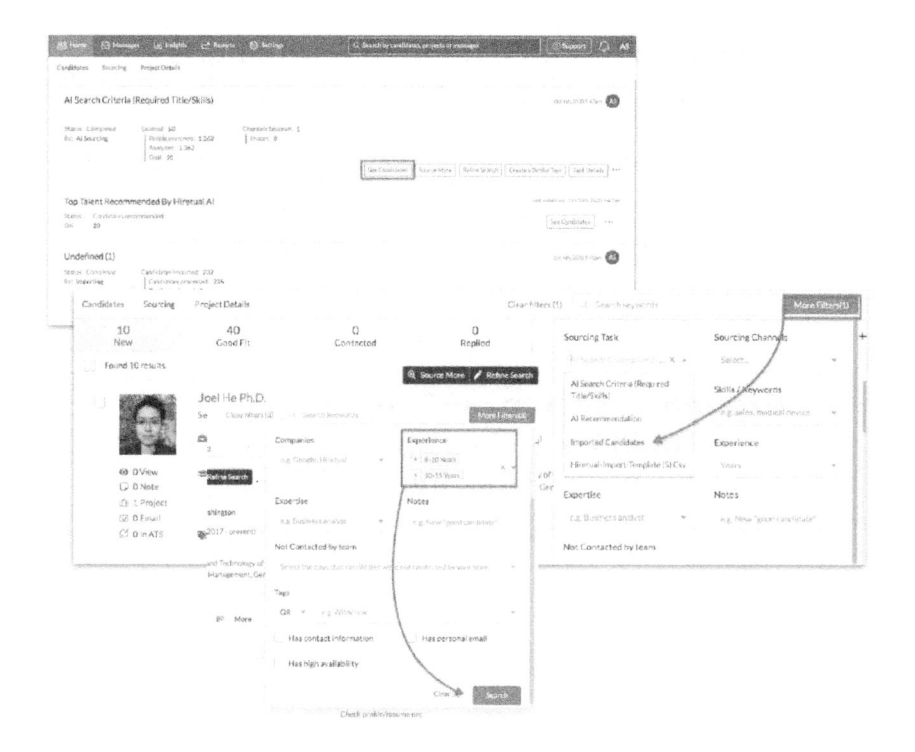

Selecting Leads that meet your Search Criteria

1. Once you finish applying the filters, decide which candidates meet your criteria. For those that are qualified, mark as a 'Good Fit' → click the candidates name to see more profile information.

2. Export candidates in CSV file from 'Good Fit' stage in Hiretual.

3. Use contact information in CSV file to reach out to candidates using preferred engagement method.

Outreach Email Sequence Campaigns
1. Simply create a project and advance these leads to the email campaign sequence stage.
2. Create sequences with recruiter templates.
3. Track each sequence and follow-up. See who opened and clicked on each message.
4. You can message someone up to 10 times within the tool.

Expanded Search on Google
When doing searches on Google, you can now see a full profile of an individual.

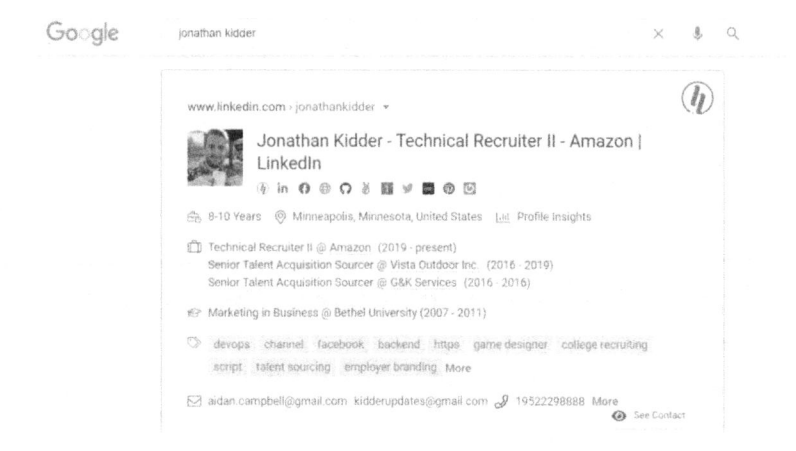

Integrated in Gmail
Track open and click rates right in Gmail. Create an email sequence with saved recruiter templates. Set reminders on follow-ups all within Gmail.

Lusha
Rating: Beginner
Features:
- Built for sales professionals in mind
- Find personal and corporate emails
- Can enrich data within CSV files
- 80-90 accuracy levels

Lusha is a top-notch tool designed to provide you with access to business-to-business (B2B) contacts and data from other companies. With this tool, you can effortlessly connect with your desired prospects and obtain their contact information within minutes. The main goal of Lusha is to assist you in gathering information about potential candidates from other companies in the B2B industry.

This tool gives you access to more than 100 million business profiles and 36 million c-level profiles, giving you the flexibility to select the right business for collaboration. You can utilize Lusha on various internet platforms, B2B sites, email platforms such as Gmail, and social media platforms like LinkedIn, Facebook, Salesforce, and others.

Getting started with Lusha is quick and easy. Simply install it as a Chrome extension and you can begin using it immediately. Once you sign up and click on the icon, you can access your prospects' contact information and the relevant details necessary for starting a sales discovery.

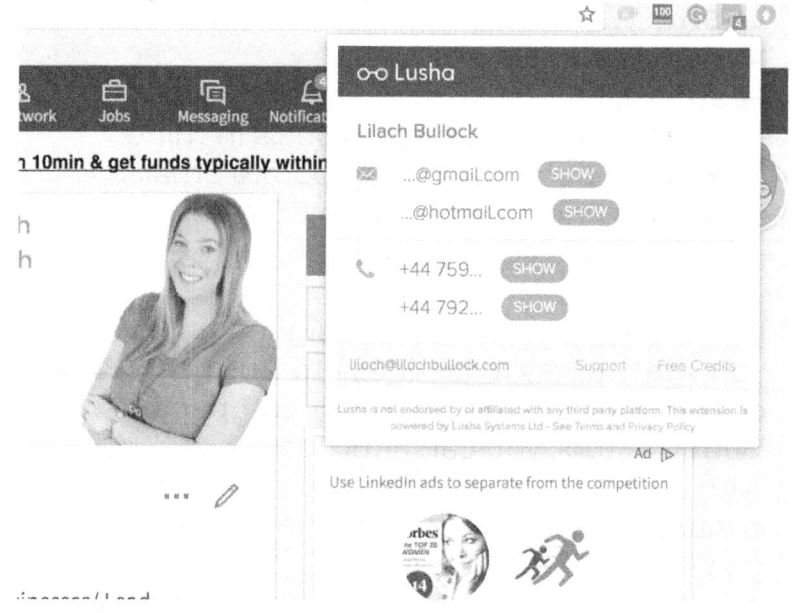

ContactOut
Rating: Beginner
Features:
- Huge database of personal emails
- Locate emails and phone numbers
- Save search and leads with the tool
- Send emails using the template feature

ContactOut boasts of having the personal emails of approximately 75% of individuals worldwide, which is truly remarkable. Like the other tools mentioned here, you can use it to search for users' personal emails and phone numbers. With its powerful features and sourcing benefits, this tool is the perfect solution for finding instant talent.

When it comes to recruitment, ContactOut is highly effective as people are more likely to open emails in their inbox than messages in their LinkedIn inbox. In fact, 85% of people prefer to communicate via email instead of LinkedIn. Obtain contact information 10 times faster than usual and use it to send an irresistible pitch and attract exceptional talent for your needs.

To start using ContactOut, simply download it as a Chrome extension. This tool also cross-references other social media platforms to expand its database of information, making it easier to locate business and personal phone numbers and email addresses.

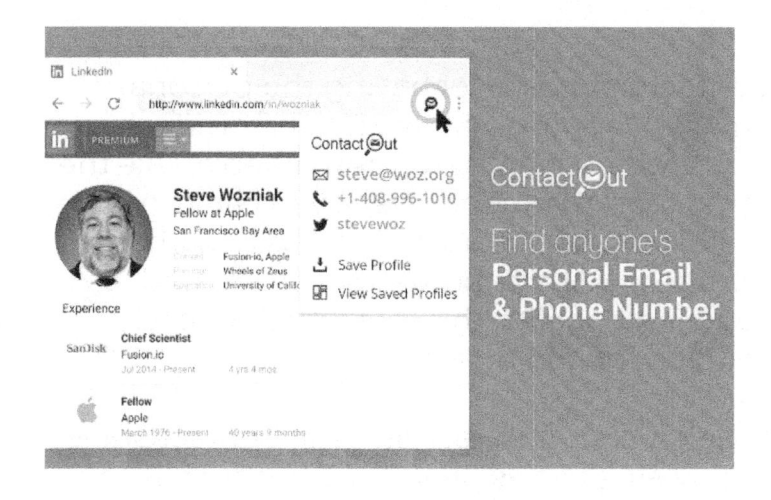

SeekOut
Rating: Advanced
Features:
- Comprehensive database
- Intuitive AI-powered search
- Auto source and rank profiles
- Diversity AI-sourcing capabilities
- Create email drip campaigns
- Talent Insights data intelligence

SeekOut has a comprehensive database and offers access to an intuitive AI search that covers whole person profiles. You can also engage professionals across industries and use personalized messaging tools for the best results. This tool is a powerful AI search engine that recruiters love to use for instant contact information and personal profile collecting.

I've been able to speak with their founder Anoop on several occasions. I'm very impressed by this extension and everything that you can do with this platform.

You can search for the complete and verified profiles on LinkedIn and GitHub and sort the candidates by project needs. Next, there is a feature where you can export the candidates list to CSV files so you can easily go through this list and choose the right candidates for your needs.

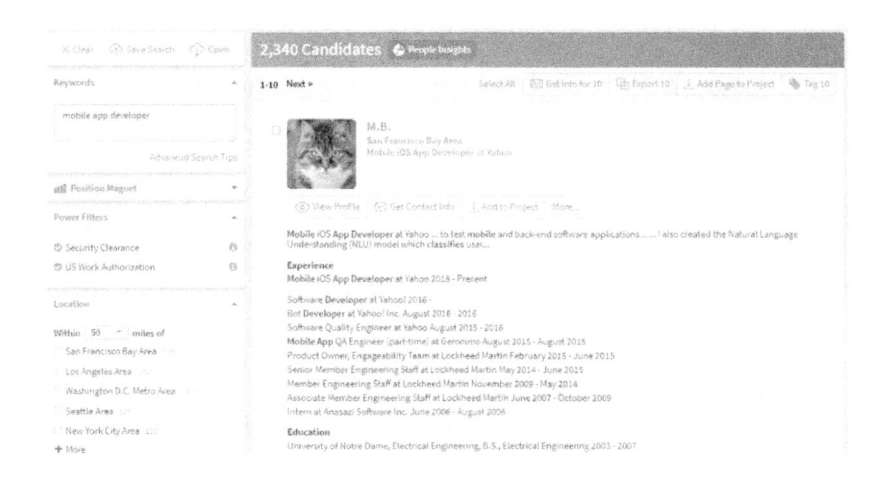

A large vast pool of Talent

Talent Pools	Description	Great for Hiring	Number of Profiles	Availability
Public Profiles	Candidates' professional experience, education, and skills from public profiles.	All roles	440M+	All SeekOut licenses
GitHub Profiles	Candidates' overall coding expertise and experience with specific programming languages based on analyzing their code and contributions to Open Source projects.	Software Engineers	15M+	Premium Tech licenses
Expert Profiles	Candidates' deep subject matter expertise based on published papers, patents, conferences, as well as metrics which measure how frequently a candidate is cited among peers.	Deep subject matter experts in technical fields, including engineering, pharmaceuticals, commerce, and machine learning	85M+	Expert licenses
Candidates in your ATS	Rediscover warm candidates from your ATS or CRM based on SeekOut's powerful search of their current profile	Great candidates that have previously applied to your company	Varies	Requires integration. Contact your SeekOut representative for details.
Employee Referrals	Identify candidates connected to your employees and easily request feedback on potential candidates directly in SeekOut	Employee Referrals	Varies	Contact your Customer Success Manager for details
37 other social and professional networks	Custom search across 37 different social, professional and technical sites from Facebook to Kaggle and more	Candidates who don't typically have professional public profiles, such as nurses, retail workers, and commercial drivers	Varies	All SeekOut licenses

53

AI Searching

With SeekOut's AI-Powered Talent Search Engine, you can search the way you want to find the candidates you need. Use machine learning and AI to find candidates who match the requirements for any job description.

Search Methods	Description	Example	Availability
Direct Search	Fast, accurate results based on keywords.	Java developer Seattle	All SeekOut licenses
Boolean Search	Full Boolean support, powerful field-based syntax, wildcards, and more to build targeted, highly precise searches.	cur_title:([radio OR antenna) AND engineer) AND (frequen* OR design)	All SeekOut licenses
Power Filters	Over 100 complex queries for in-demand roles available with a single click.	☑ Front-end Frameworks ☑ MachineLearning	All SeekOut licenses
AI Matching	Automatically find great candidates that match your job descriptions.	Find best fit candidates from any JD	All SeekOut licenses
Diversity Search Filters	Take actionable, specific steps to improve diversity in your organization by finding and including highly qualified, diverse candidates in your recruiting pipelines.	Search filters for female, Hispanic, Black or African American, and veteran candidates	All SeekOut licenses
Enhanced Clearance Filters	5 times more cleared candidate search results than any other tool, with the industry's most precise control over clearance level searches.	12 precise levels of clearance and access filtering	Expert Licenses, or Premium Tech Licenses with Enhanced Clearance Filters upgrade. Requires activation. Contact your SeekOut representative for details.
Custom Power Filters	Custom Power Filters designed to improve your team's efficiency and meet the specific recruiting needs of your organization.	Custom	Speak with your Customer Success Manager to understand available options for Custom Power Filters.

Talent Pool Insights

Analyze the frequency or scarcity of specific skill sets and backgrounds, the geographic distribution of talent, and where candidates currently and previously worked. Use these insights to build an actionable recruiting strategy, benchmark against your competition, and more.

Engage Candidates

Contact candidates using highly verified phone numbers and emails and improve candidate response rate with automated, integrated, and personalized email engagement.

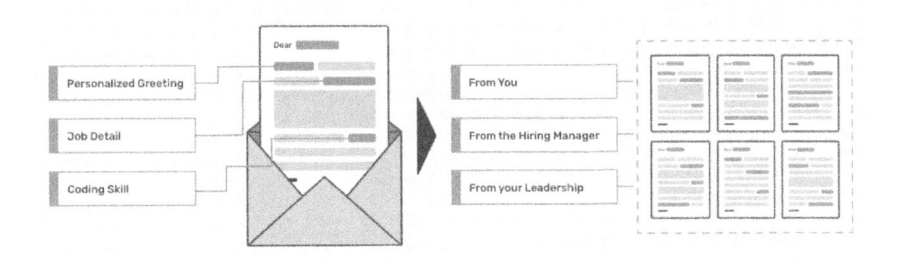

Find highly qualified diverse candidates

Take action to improve diversity in your organization by finding and including highly qualified, diverse candidates in your recruiting pipelines. SeekOut's diversity search filters for female, Hispanic, Black or African American, and veteran candidates which deliver up to five times as many highly qualified diverse candidates as other recruiting tools.

Expanded search on Google

When conducting a search, SeekOut will expand individual profiles.

Within each profile, there will be keyword tags included. Scroll over each keyword to get a

55

definition. This will help improve your sourcing abilities.

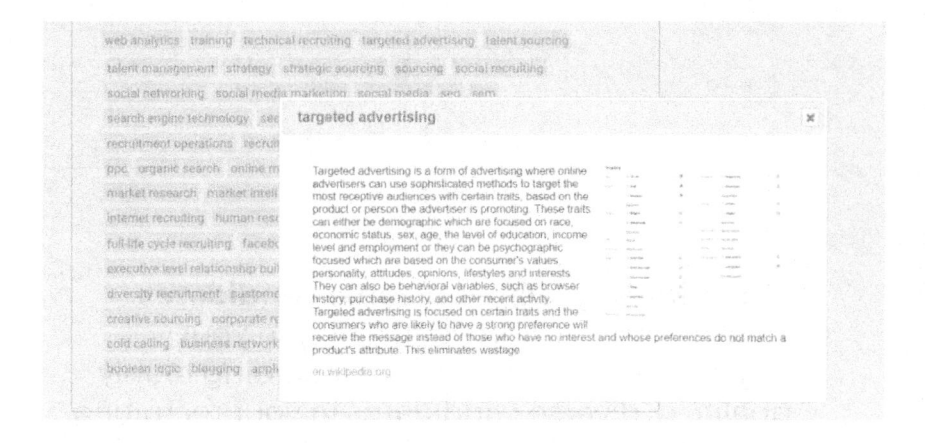

HiringSolved

Rating: Advanced
Features:

- Massive database of users
- Consolidated Profiles
- Technical Pre-Screen matching
- Search passive talent

HiringSolved is an award-winning, AI recruiting software that helps professional recruiters with amazing workflow and team focus in the process of talent searching. Using this tool, you can upgrade your team productivity and automate some processes like sourcing and outsourcing, engagement, and more. Therefore, retaining the right candidate for your business needs no matter how much time you want to contract them.

You get a lot of features using HiringSolved; one of them is the ability to unify HR data. This feature will allow you to unify CRM, HRIS and ATS with one search interface. There will be real-time business insights too, so your wanted candidates will be perfectly matched with their job experiences.

Also, this tool is offering automation processes where the recruiting team can easily connect and focus on the workflow as well as the human steps during the recruiting process. The historical hiring trends and market insights can be supervised live, so that's how you will benefit looking for the right people in the right time.

HiringSolved is a free recruiting tool based on AI, so you just need to sign up on their official site and make yourself an account. Then, search for a specific keyword or job description and the list of potential candidates will appear on the screen, together with their information.

AmazingHiring
Rating: Intermediate
Features:
- Massive Database of Users
- Consolidated Profiles
- Technical Pre-Screen matching
- Search passive talent pools
- GDPR compliant: Great tool for International markets

AmazingHiring is the ultimate search engine for finding technical talent. They have over a million profiles in their database. If you're mainly focused on finding tech talent, this would be a great tool to use. It has a simple user-friendly dashboard that allows you to add keywords to quickly create a Boolean search.

Their database of users is pretty impressive and with a quick search, I was able to find a list of iOS developers without having to use LinkedIn. They were then easily able to respond to my introduction email. Hopefully, AmazingHiring will continue to add users, optimize their consolidated profiles, pre-screen matches, and include more social media sites in the future. It will be interesting to see how AI technology will play into this search engine tool.

This tool allows you to research more than 600 million profiles, more than LinkedIn, which is awesome for faster talent researching and recruiting. Also, AmazingHiring will allow you to get a list of potential candidates according to your keyword research, collecting them into pipeline. There is a chance for you to contact the candidates from the list using live chat, which is a big advantage over competitors.

Installing this Chrome extension is really easy, and you can do it with one click in the

Chrome extension field. This is a free tool you will activate with one click on the icon, where it shows a list of candidates with their information – location, name and surname, skills – thanks to the search engine plugin.

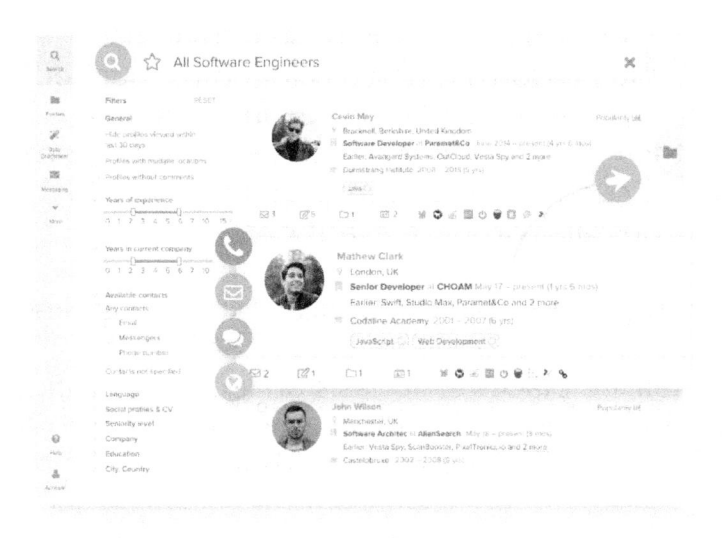

SignalHire
Rating: Advanced
Features:
- Advanced candidate search tool
- Built-in CRM tracking features
- Market labor analytics
- A feature-rich contact finding Chrome extension
- Tools can find contact details from CSV files
- Accuracy levels range from 50-60 percent

SignalHire provides a suite of tools including candidate search, recruitment job search, market statistics, and tracking capabilities. The company has also launched an extension tool to enhance its functionality.

The extension allows you to search across multiple platforms such as LinkedIn, Facebook, Twitter, Meetup, and Google+ for personal contact information. You can also find personal details such as website information, Indeed resumes, and other relevant data.

In comparison to other similar extensions like HireEz, Lusha, Connectifier, and SeekOut, SignalHire places emphasis on locating verified emails and contact information. The app provides this information firsthand.

SignalHire is a paid tool, but it offers a free trial for users to test its features. During the trial, you will receive five email credits per month and access to search over 450 million profiles in the database. For $39 per month, you can get up to 350 email credits.

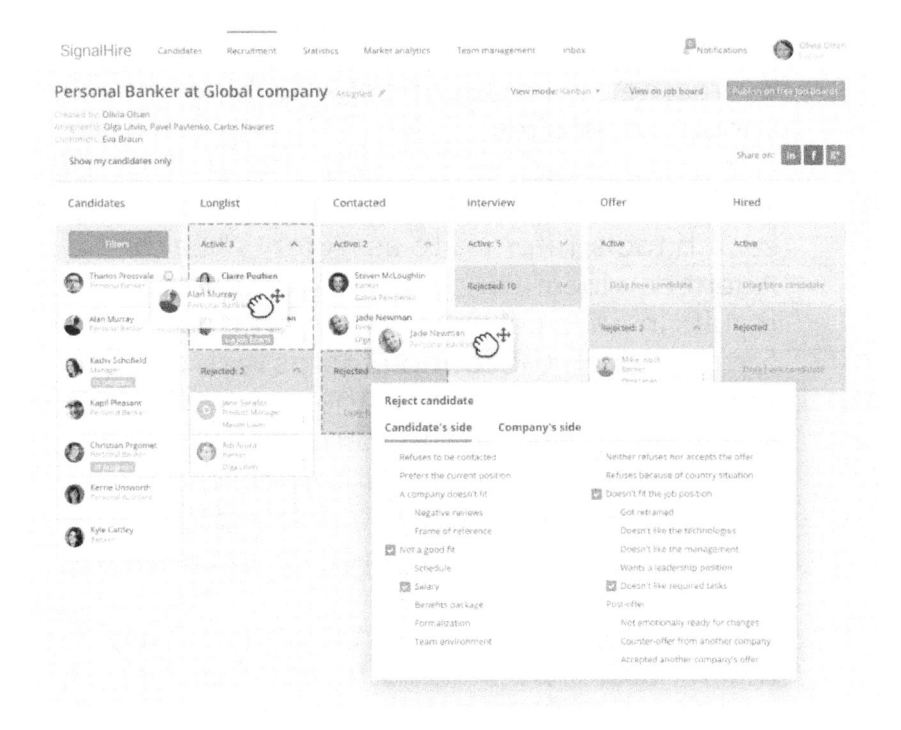

Social List
Rating: Intermediate
Features:
- Search by name, company name, domain, or URL profile
- Find email addresses and phone numbers
- Easily scrape profiles and build large CSV lists

Social List is a tool that enables you to quickly generate lists of targeted social profiles that match your desired criteria, such as locations, employers, and job titles. Its search function is more precise and robust than traditional x-ray search engine methods and helps you overcome the limitations of searching on various social sites.

The tool comprises of several site-specific search tools, referred to as "Agents." Each Agent can locate and save up to 100 search results in an Excel file, and Social List can further enrich the found records with email addresses. The Social List Agents have been developed based on the company's accumulated expertise in internet search behavior, incorporating multiple search parameters to deliver high-precision results.

Social List is a paid tool, but it offers a 7-day free trial for users to test its features. After the trial, the tool costs $529 per year (or $49 per month) with a maximum of 500 daily searches.

You can also export the lists in an Excel document (up to 300 per day) with 120 enrichment credits available throughout the year.

> Welcome to Social List 1.0
>
> LinkedIn Agent
> Precise Member Search by Company, Role, Location, Certification Abbreviation, or Name
>
> Zoominfo Agent
> Precise Profile Search by Company, Role, Address, Country, or Name
>
> Meetup Agent
> Precise Member Search by Location, Meetup Name
>
> Github Agent #001
> Precise Profile Search by Name, Location, Company, or Email Domain
>
> Github Agent #002
> Precise Profile Search - Repositories (by Languages) and Location
>
> Google Plus Agent
> Precise Profile Search by Name, Location, Company, Email Domain

SalesQL

Rating: Beginner

Features:

- Contact finding extension tool
- Enriches data from CSV files
- Created for Sales B2B leads

SalesQL is an extension tool that helps find contact information from LinkedIn users. It helps find phone numbers and email addresses for your LinkedIn connections. Easily download your LinkedIn connections and extract their contact details in bulk, direct from LinkedIn search pages – great for building prospect databases and networking lists.

Download all your LinkedIn connections:
LinkedIn recently blocked this feature for users to download all their connections with contact

details. Thankfully, you can use this tool to download all your connections, and as a huge bonus, it will enrich those contact details with all known information.

Pricing Structure:
Honestly, it's quite competitively priced compared to other competing extensions. I would recommend using this tool if you are new to the contact finding tools world.

Starter: $39 (1,500 Credits / Month)
Advanced: $59 (4,000 Credits / Month)
Pro: $89 (10,000 Credits / Month)

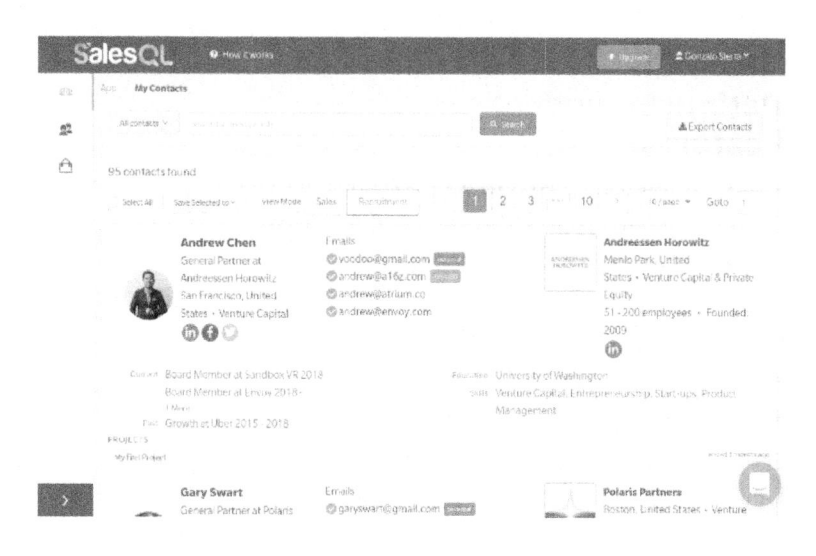

developerDB
Rating: Intermediate
Features:
- Great for searching on GitHub or Stack Overflow
- Gives you the tech stack off tech profiles
- 60-70 percent accuracy levels

developerDB is a great extension to find and source tech talent online. Reach more passive candidates and sales prospects with a database of 30 million tech workers. This database consists of a wide range of tech people, many not found elsewhere, along with tech-specialized data that enables better targeting. I've had full access to this tool for a while and I can say that I'm truly impressed by its features.

developerDB is Not a Traditional Data Provider
Traditional data providers are good at basic business information: Name, business email, job title, and company location. They are convenient as they cover broad ranges of industries but are not good for reaching tech people.

- There are no profiles of non-traditional tech people: ex. Freelancers, contract, or career changers.
- Traditional data is lacking deep coverage in most tech niche areas.

- No tech specific data such as tech skill rankings and "beyond work" tech activities.
- Outdated information: Data is refreshed quarterly or longer.

Platform and Chrome Extension
- Find developer's tech stacks, expertise, and repositories.
- All the information needed for first contact! Users keep the data they want.
- Find the personal emails, social media, and work information online.
- Tech Rankings on various tech skills.

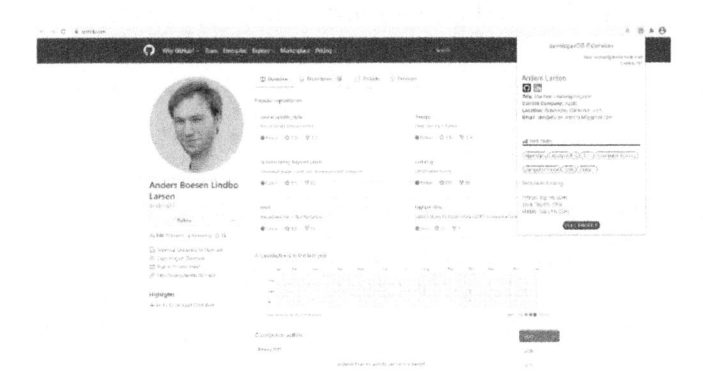

jobin
Rating: Intermediate
Features:
- Webscraping integration
- Email and inmail automation
- Contacting finding extension

Jobin is a comprehensive automation platform that streamlines the sales and recruitment efforts on LinkedIn. With numerous features, including scraping, email verification, data finding and enrichment, bulk email automation with mail merge, and many more, this tool helps to make your work more efficient and productive.

Efficiently sort through profiles by method of contact data. Having a large number of contacts is useful, but if they cannot be easily reached, then it is not very valuable. Jobin understands the importance of this, which is why we have created a specific filter for this purpose. All filters have a corresponding exclude option, including: Email, Mobile phone number, Landline phone number, Website, and social media profiles.

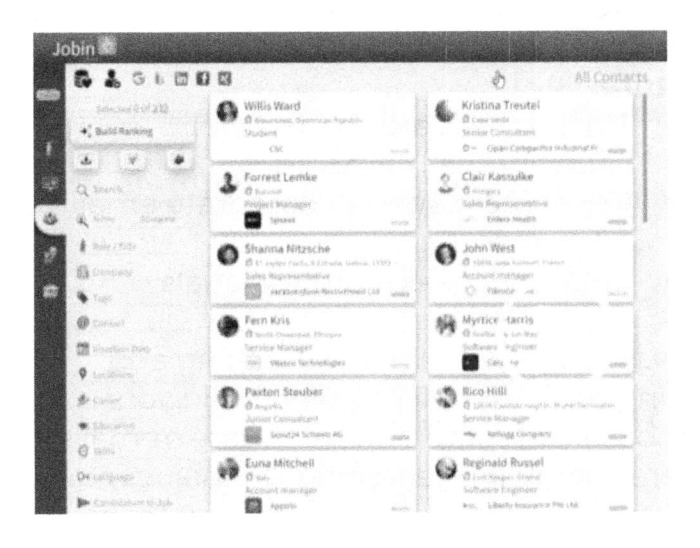

Chapter 4: Email Tools

If you're looking for someone's email address, using a sales or recruitment tool is your best option. By using these tools as extensions on web pages, you can easily uncover all email addresses associated with a domain and all verified emails of your desired prospects on social media and other online platforms.

Why Do You Need Email Tools?
Email tracking is legal under GDPR if your organization complies with GDPR. Compliance depends on your organization's relationship with the recipients of your emails. Using email tools will help you track, find, and locate verified emails around the web. Using such extensions will save you a lot of time and effort during the recruiting process.

Snov.io
Rating: Beginner
Features:
- Track emails around the web
- Launch email campaigns
- 100 percent verified corporate email addresses
- Created for sales professionals

Snov.io is a powerful email tracking and finding tool that will help you build your database with potential candidate's emails wherever you are searching for their contact information. As a professional recruiter, using this tool will boost the process of finding and generating leads on the web, with the availability to launch email marketing campaigns and collect emails from potential talent.

You can get this Chrome extension for free by searching for Snov.io. You can install it with one click and the tool icon will appear. Launch the extension with one click. Just go to the website or social media platform (preferably LinkedIn) where you want to search for top tier candidates and click the Snov.io icon in the extensions.

There will be a list of their verified personal or business emails which can be used to contact them for collaboration. This will save you time and effort and allow you to focus on other important tasks that are a part of the recruiting process.

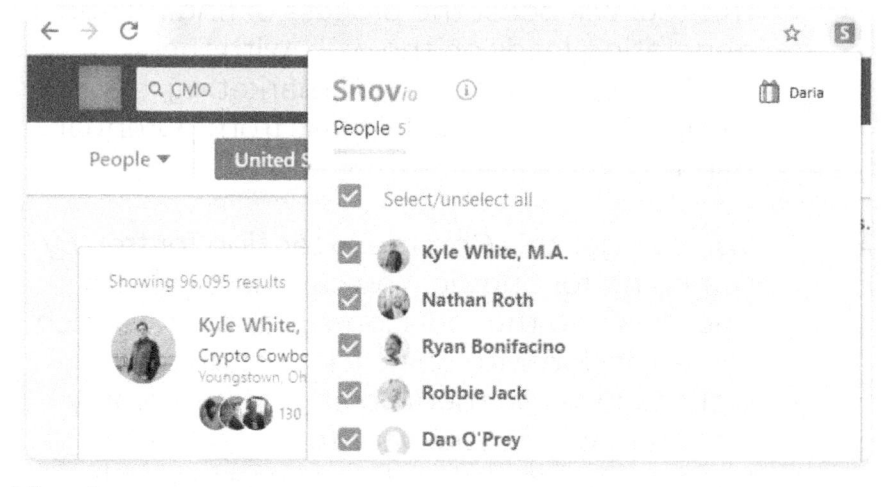

Hunter
Rating: Beginner
Features:
- Leading solution for email finding
- Only gives you verified email results
- Full Domain search
- Integrates with Gmail and Outlook as an email tracking tool

Hunter is a domain search tool that enables you to find verified emails of individuals or businesses from various sources across the web. As a recruiter, you can easily access over 100 million email addresses, along with the names and companies of your desired candidates. Hunter is a leading email-finding tool in the market and is a crucial component in your recruitment and talent sourcing processes.

One of its beneficial features is the ability to find and reach out to candidates in bulk and gather their contact information into a database, which can be done in just a matter of minutes due to Hunter's speedy algorithm. Finding emails has never been easier, but with this email verifier, you can also determine which emails are valid and which are not, ensuring you always have access to a real email address that you can use confidently for your recruitment efforts.

Hunter offers both a free and paid option. The free plan allows you to perform 50 searches and email verifications per month, while the starter package provides 500 searches and verifications for $49 per month. The pro package, which costs $199 per month, offers 10,000 searches and verifications each month.

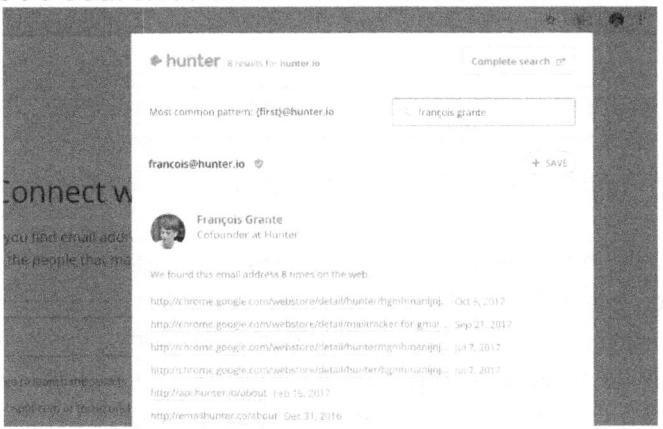

FindEmails.com (Formerly Toofr)
Rating: Beginner
Features:

- Email addresses can be found using bulk lists
- Chrome plugin available for increased convenience

FindEmails is a website that finds company email addresses using the name of an individual, company, or website. The site skims through several million mail servers and business email patterns to deliver results.

You can request FindEmails to find the email details of a single person or entity or get the email addresses in bulk. In case you want the site to find more than a handful of email addresses, you can send in the inputs as a spreadsheet. Based on the plan chosen, FindEmails can process a minimum of 100 records every hour.

You can buy lists with verified data from other members with similar targets and business goals as you in the marketplace or put up your own and make a few extra bucks.

FindEmails discovers business email addresses from the first and last names and the company name or website. It uses millions of business email patterns and mail server results to give you industry leading sending rates. Unfortunately, this is not a free tool, so using FindEmails will require you roughly $29 - $99 depending on the package size.

Using this tool is really easy. Just go to the official website and install it as a Chrome extension. Then, in the search section of the tool, fill in the gaps to get certain information about the candidate that you are looking for. There is an option to write the name and the surname of the candidate together with the company he/she operates and to find just their email. This is a powerful feature if you are targeting candidates already known to you but don't have their contact information.

Webdef
Rating: Beginner
Features:
- Syncs contacts with CRM
- LinkedIn features
- Verified emails only

Using Webdef, you will be able to find verified emails and direct-dial phone numbers of contacts on LinkedIn, and sync them with your CRM instantly. Beyond LinkedIn, you can find contacts from potential candidates all around the web, including their name and surname, phone number, email address, where they are living, and an accompanying profile picture if it is available.

The huge benefit of using this Chrome extension is the availability to sync your new contacts with your existing ones creating a massive list of verified emails. Webdef is free, and you can use it whenever you want, with just one click on the Chrome extension icon.

GetEmail.io
Rating: Beginner
Features:
- Fast research
- Easy to use interface
- Free Chrome extension

GetEmail.io is the easiest way to find email addresses from anywhere on the web, with just one click. GetEmail.io is a magic tool that finds the professional email address of anyone, whatever their company or position.

According to the results, GetEmail has the highest success rate of finding emails and the lowest email bounce rate on the market. This tool was created by two top-tier French engineers who applied advanced big data and machine learning algorithms to deliver such a high quality of service.

Using this tool, you can get any email by clicking the Chrome extension icon when you open up a specific platform or website. You will get a list of potential clients ready for recruiting with their phone numbers, email addresses, full name and picture included. GetEmail is a free tool, but there are packages you can pay for more intensive use and additional features.

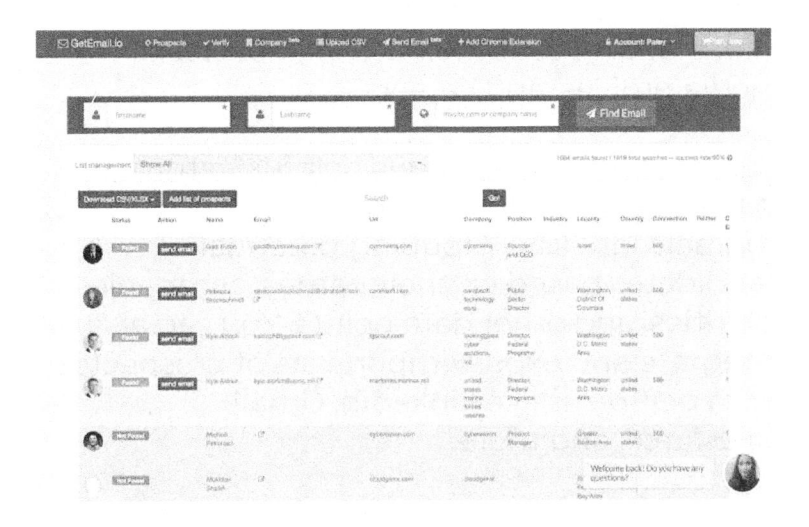

GetProspect
Rating: Intermediate
Features:
- Integration from many platforms
- Invite your team for recruiting
- Exporting option in XLS

GetProspect is a powerful tool for recruiters and email hunters that is widely used by professionals in the talent research field. Simply enter your search criteria, and the GetProspect email extractor will provide you with a list of names with corporate email addresses, job titles, LinkedIn profile URLs, company names, industries, and websites, among other information.

With its user-friendly interface, recruiters can easily track down their desired prospects and find their contact information, along with information about their companies, social media profiles, and careers.

GetProspect offers various helpful features, including the ability to categorize your contacts into lists, grouping potential candidates based on their names, companies, job titles, and other data points. You can also integrate and export/import lists of prospects from platforms like LinkedIn, Gmail, Salesforce, and more.

Exporting files in XLS format is also available for bulk email imports and company information. This tool is a paid service, but you can start with a free trial. The free pricing plan allows for 100 email searches per month. The starter package offers 1000 searches and verifications per month for $49.

For $99 per month, you can access up to 5000 email searches and verifications.

Getting started with GetProspect is simple. Just sign up and create an account. In the search bar, enter a specific name or keyword that matches a profession. You will receive a list of potential prospects, complete with their email addresses, phone numbers, company information, social media links, and locations.

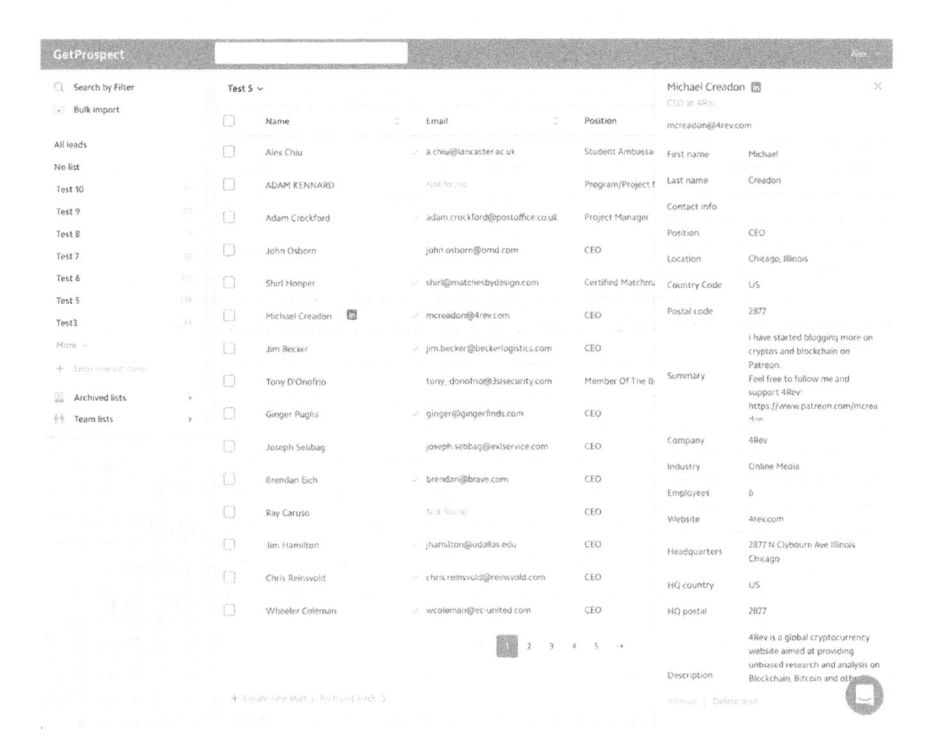

LeadIQ
Rating: Beginner
Features:
- Use it across different platforms
- Find contact information using LinkedIn profiles
- 90 percent accuracy levels

LeadIQ allows you to prospect effortlessly as you browse LinkedIn or any other website.

77

With a single click, you can send the contact information of your desired lead to all your preferred sales tools, such as Salesforce, Outreach, SalesLoft, and more. Over 10,000 industries rely on LeadIQ to track potential prospects, streamline sales, and gather crucial data like contact information. The LeadIQ dashboard provides managers with an overview of their team's prospecting activities.

Streamline the connection between prospecting and closed deals with just one click. To get started, simply sign up for a new profile on the official website and start utilizing this effective recruiting tool.

LeadIQ is committed to integrating with various sales software to ensure that your leads reach their destination with just one click. The data is frequently updated, so you always have access to the latest information.

For a monthly fee of $75, you can expand your team and recruit up to three licensed members with the help of this paid tool.

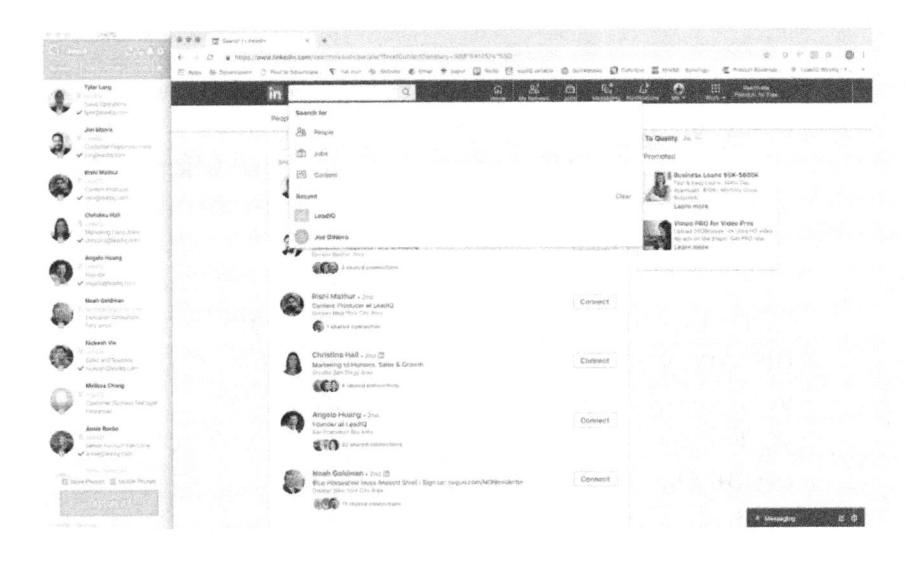

LeadLeaper
Rating: Beginner
Features:
- Integration with Microsoft Office 365
- Tracking email history
- Email signatures

LeadLeaper is a Chrome extension you can use to discover a lead's email address. When you see a promising LinkedIn profile and want to find the candidate's email address, just open the icon in the extension field and watch the magic happen.

LeadLeaper LinkedIn email finder adds the new lead to your list, including a verified business email address and since LeadLeaper always remembers which emails you previously discovered, there are no duplicates and an email never counts twice.

This tool will allow you to send emails and track your leads. Employ LeadLeaper's integration with Google G Suite and Microsoft Office 365 to send thousands of personalized emails monthly.

With LeadLeaper's open tracking and email history, you're notified whenever a lead opens your email and you always know what emails you've sent to each lead. Included are custom email signatures, unsubscribe links, and reusable email templates.

There are over 60,000 users worldwide, which shows a trustworthiness among users. Installing and using this tool is quite simple, just install it as a Chrome extension to get started.

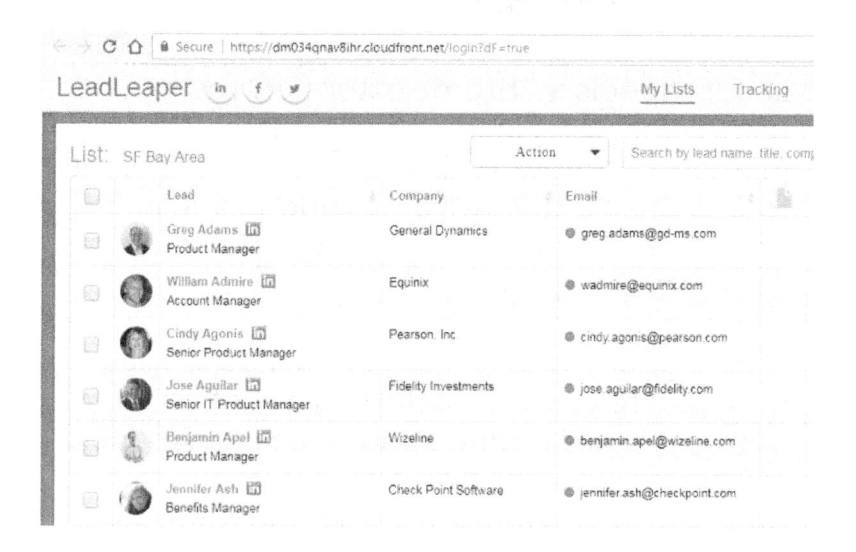

Skrapp
Rating: Beginner
Features:
- LinkedIn and Sales Navigator email finder
- Company domain email finder
- Bulk email finder
- Built-in email verifier

Trustful data and productivity are essential measures. Skrapp.io is an out-of-the-box tool that helps you find verified B2B email addresses of people that matter for your business. Whether it's through LinkedIn, company websites, or using the in-app features, this tool will help you build the email list for your next outreach campaign.

Skrapp.io is a leading SaaS company in the B2B email research industry. Through the set of features and services available, you will be able to find email marketing professionals to build relevant B2B email lists.

The best feature on Skrapp.io is the domain search. This is an advanced search feature. It allows you to find employee's emails from their company's website. The Domain Search Chrome feature relies on the Domain Search service, which pulls from a database of millions of emails.

This is an easy-to-use Chrome extension and installing it is a really easy process. Skrapp.io is a paid app, but you can use it for free too. The free trial will give you 150 email searches per month.

The starter pack costs $39 per month. You get 1000 email searches with up to two members from your recruiting team.

The seeker package cost $79. You get 5000 email searches per month and the option to include five other team members.

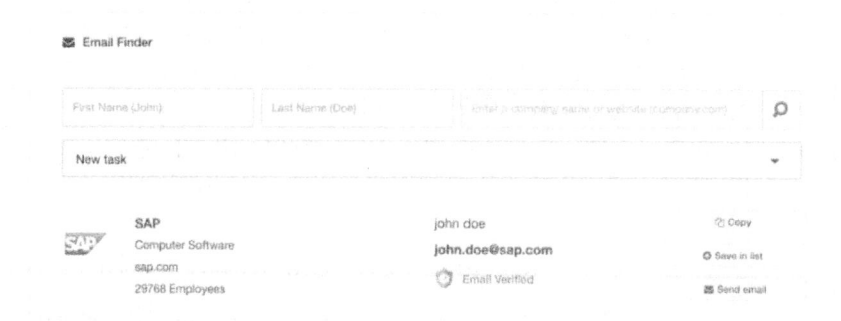

WhoKnows
Rating: Intermediate
Features:
- Powerful search engine
- Make your own dashboard
- Integration in different platforms

WhoKnows is a newer tool that has multiple capabilities. To start with, it is a sourcing tool that also has over 307 million candidate databases. These candidates are worldwide and ready to go. In addition, using its browser extension will allow you to grab candidates from sites and add them to your list/folder of potential candidates.

The 307 million profiles it has amassed come from multiple places, including LinkedIn. They have gone out and captured all public LinkedIn profiles, enhanced them and created a database.

They are pitching themselves as a true LinkedIn alternative. That said, they are looking into and starting to grow their database with profiles from other sites such as: GitHub, Stack Overflow, Facebook, Twitter, and more.

WhoKnows has invented a patented, machine-learning discovery platform that automatically derives expertise and relationships to generate semantic, detailed, always up-to-date profiles and connections.

Their basic limited search features are free as a Chrome extension. This is perfect if you want to get familiar with the platform before committing or if you just need it to supplement other tools. There are various levels that include access to all the features, and each includes a free trial.

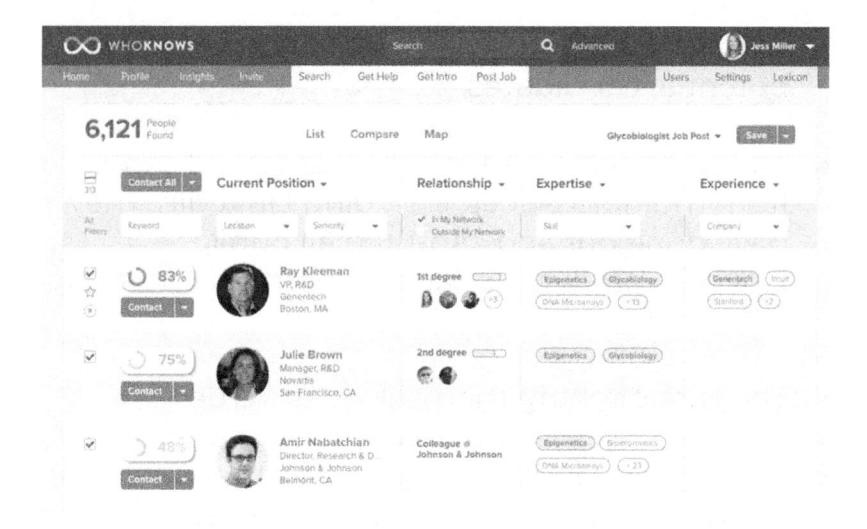

Anymail Finder

Rating: Beginner

Features:
- Search leads based on Job titles
- Bulk searching
- Find real emails or they are free

Anymail Finder is a powerful tool that helps you find and verify email addresses with ease. With Anymail Finder, you only pay for 100% verified emails, so you can be confident that they won't bounce. If the tool can't verify an email, it's free. The server sends a positive response, indicating that the mailbox exists, ensuring that you receive real emails with a bounce rate of less than 3%. Duplicate emails are never charged, so you can upload the same file as many times as you like without incurring any additional costs. You can even add unlimited team members to your account. If you only need to use Anymail Finder once, you don't have to subscribe. Simply pay for the emails in your file.

With Anymail Finder's bulk upload feature, you can upload a file of up to 50,000 rows and convert them into emails. Most email finders require you to know the website, but with Anymail Finder, you can upload a CSV file containing only the company name and receive emails. This is a huge advantage as many services only provide an email address and then charge you extra to verify it. With Anymail Finder, verification and email retrieval are done simultaneously, making it a popular choice among users.

Imagine being able to obtain the email address of someone who has tweeted about wanting your product. This is possible with Anymail Finder. Simply download tweets shared on BuzzSumo and upload them using the bulk tool. This feature works on any social media platform, so keep that in mind. Anymail Finder is free to use, and you only pay for advanced features such as verified emails. The tool is simple to use - simply type keywords into the search bar, and the results will appear, just like other tools.

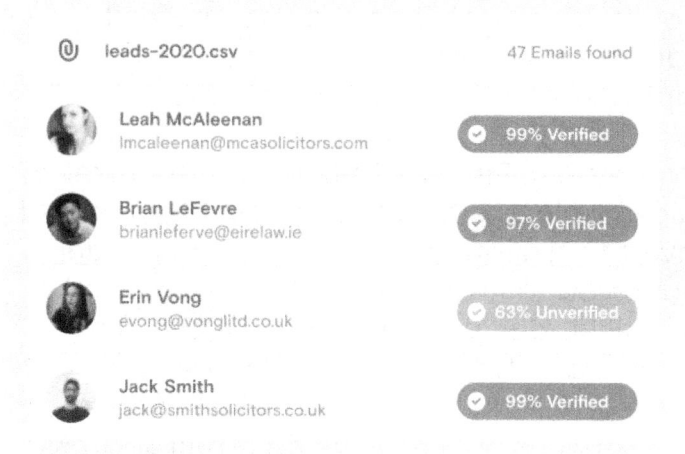

📎	leads-2020.csv		47 Emails found
👤	Leah McAleenan lmcaleenan@mcasolicitors.com		✓ 99% Verified
👤	Brian LeFevre brianleferve@eirelaw.ie		✓ 97% Verified
👤	Erin Vong evong@vonglitd.co.uk		✓ 63% Unverified
👤	Jack Smith jack@smithsolicitors.co.uk		✓ 99% Verified

Discoverly

Rating: Beginner
Features:
- Search for profiles with information on Facebook and LinkedIn
- Integrates with Gmail like Sales Navigator
- Free option and simple to use

Reveal, and now save, more complete social contact information alongside those online profiles you normally view. Gmail, Facebook, Twitter and LinkedIn don't often play well together, but Discoverly helps them play nice. This is an amazing tool for finding emails and candidates on social media platforms together with their contact information.

- Gmail: see contacts work information, mutual connections and tweets

- LinkedIn profiles: see when you have mutual Facebook friends and tweets.
- Facebook profiles: see LinkedIn information, mutual connections and tweets
- Twitter profiles: see LinkedIn information, mutual connections from Facebook and LinkedIn

Great for a job hunter, sales person, recruiter, entrepreneur, or anyone looking to find an email address. Discoverly is a free Chrome extension and you can use it whenever you want on the web and social media too.

Go to the Chrome extension and click the tool icon. Then open up any of your social media profiles and there will be a list of some potential candidates with their contact information and personal information such as name and surname, a picture of them, their location and email address along with their various social media profiles on other platforms.

You can then use this information to pitch them and contact them for future collaboration.

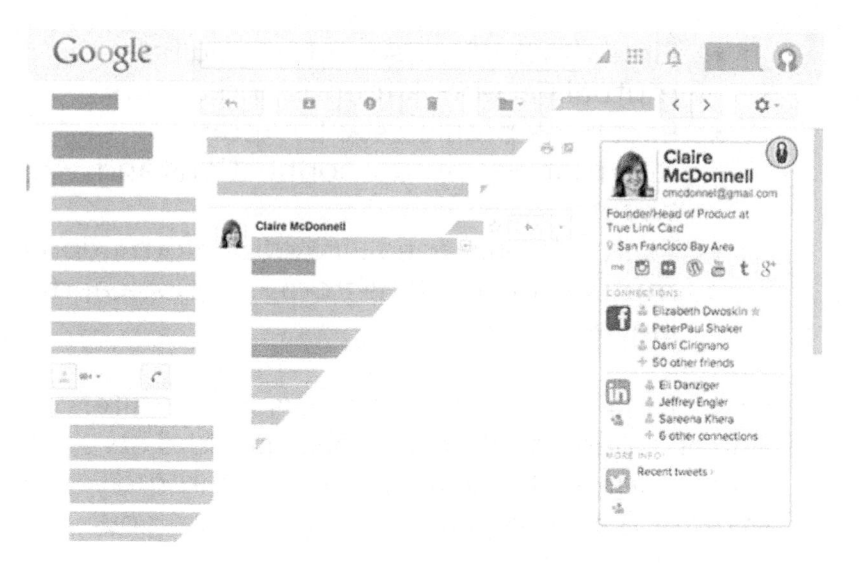

Chapter 5: Email Verification and Deliverability Tools

Email remains one of the most preferred and effective modes of communication, with most individuals checking their inboxes on a daily basis. However, a significant percentage of collected email addresses, around 10-20%, are inaccurate due to human error.

In a recent consumer survey, over 70 percent of global consumers check their email more than once a day. So, the email tools that provide real and verified email address have crucial importance in the recruiting sector.

Why Do You Need Email Verification Tools?

Real leads start with real emails, and the use of email validation is still the most effective way to ensure the collection of quality data. When you verify email addresses, your email marketing is more effective, fraud prevention is improved, and the ability to protect your sender reputation increases.

Verify Email
Rating: Beginner
Features:

- Email ID checker
- Find only verified emails on the web
- Reach out to real people with real email addresses

Verify Email is a powerful email verifier and checker for trusted email verification services since 2010. This tool constantly strives to enhance your email-verified list and improves your personal experience to verify an email address online.

This tool has helped countless numbers of email list brokers, email marketers, data centers, call centers, and lead generation groups for years. It helps check your email lists and reduces your bounce rate.

Many users find this free checker feature useful, while others opt to use the bulk checker for larger lists. This one is a powerful feature, especially if you have a large list with email addresses and you are not sure if they are 100 percent valid.

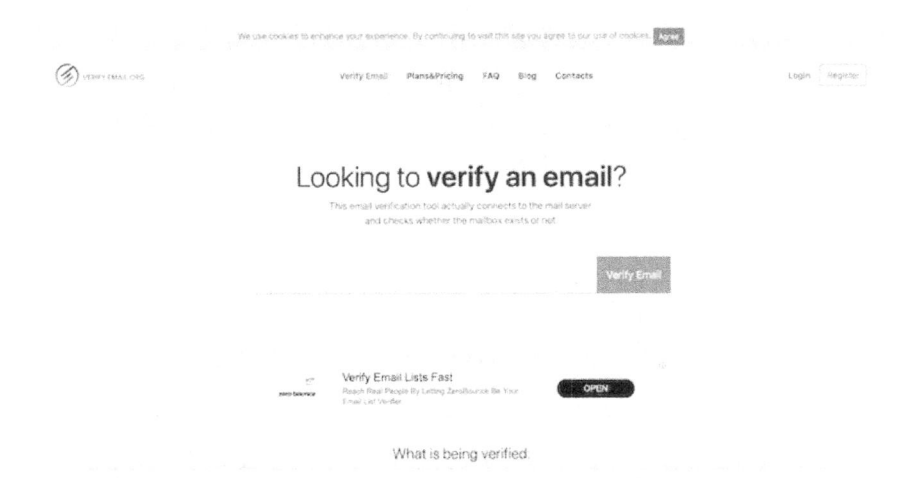

FindThatLead

Rating: Beginner
Features:
- Lead generation
- Social media search
- Prospector

With FindThatLead, you can effortlessly find any email address you need on LinkedIn and other web domains, connect with key decision makers, expand your network, and drive business growth.

Discover and verify emails from any website or LinkedIn profile in just a matter of seconds. Seamlessly transition from researching a lead to verifying their email and sending a message, all without ever having to leave your browser.

Moreover, use the Chrome extension to effortlessly export your newly found leads into mailing lists and create email drip campaigns for maximum impact.

FindThatLead is a streamlined lead generation solution that offers cutting-edge features for today's top teams - no more wasting time with manual searches on Google and social media.

Take advantage of numerous features that will streamline your recruitment process, including:

Lead search: Easily search for specific new leads.
Business emails: Quickly obtain authentic business emails of new leads at any company by simply providing their first and last name, along with website information.
Email verifier: Verify emails within seconds, eliminating the uncertainty of bounced emails with the help of the advanced algorithm.
Email sender: Create highly effective email campaigns. Let FindThatLead assist in building a targeted campaign and sending it to your leads, complete with all the necessary sales funnels and analytics for performance assessment and business growth.
Social search: Leverage social media accounts. Convert LinkedIn, Instagram, and more profiles into verified email leads.

Prospector: Locate the prospects you need with ease. Select from audience segments such as location and keywords, and reach millions of qualified leads with ease.

FindThatLead enables you to build hyper-targeted lists of your ideal candidates, reducing manual sourcing time and increasing opportunities to connect with new talents and acquire more customers.

Acquire thousands of verified emails and social profiles daily to power your cold outreach campaigns and fuel your growth hacking experiments. Easily find, export, and upload them to your funnels in minutes.

Get started by installing the Chrome extension from the official website and creating a free account. Simply upload your email list, and the tool will show you which email addresses are valid and which are not.

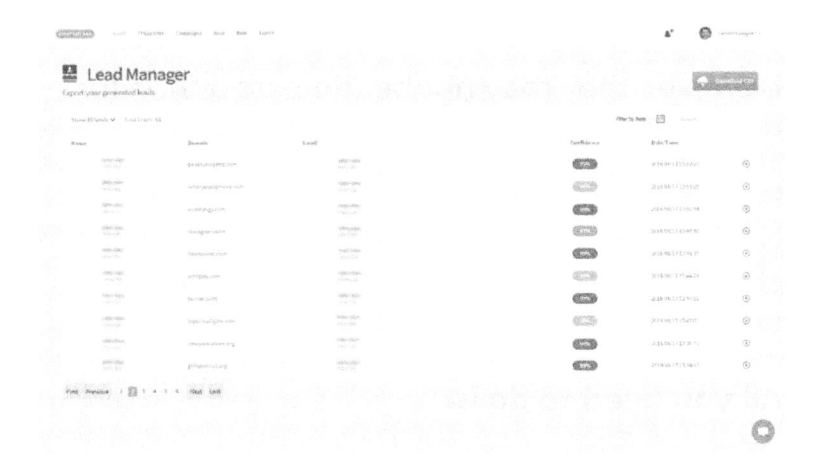

EmailListVerify

Rating: Beginner
Features:
- Good Verification Accuracy (80 percent)
- The minimum order value is only $4 for 1000 email credits
- Integrates with leading ESPs

EmailListVerify is a trusted email validation tool and service provider, renowned for its effective management and validation of substantial email lists, with an accuracy rate of 85%. They offer two flexible options to choose from, either a pay-as-you-go plan or a monthly subscription for regular campaigns, depending on your specific needs.

EmailListVerify also provides free resources such as an email health checker to evaluate your DNS, DMARC records, and configurations. With their real-time verification API, they can verify up to 100,000 emails per month for just $169.

However, they may not be the best option for those seeking automation in email list cleaning, as their offerings in this area may seem limited. But for large-scale email verification, EmailListVerify is an excellent choice and is praised for its efficiency in the task.

All you need to do is:

1. Create an account and get 100 email verifications for free.
2. Upload your dirty list. CSV, XLS, TXT and other formats are accepted.
3. Download a clean list. You will be notified within a few minutes with verified emails.

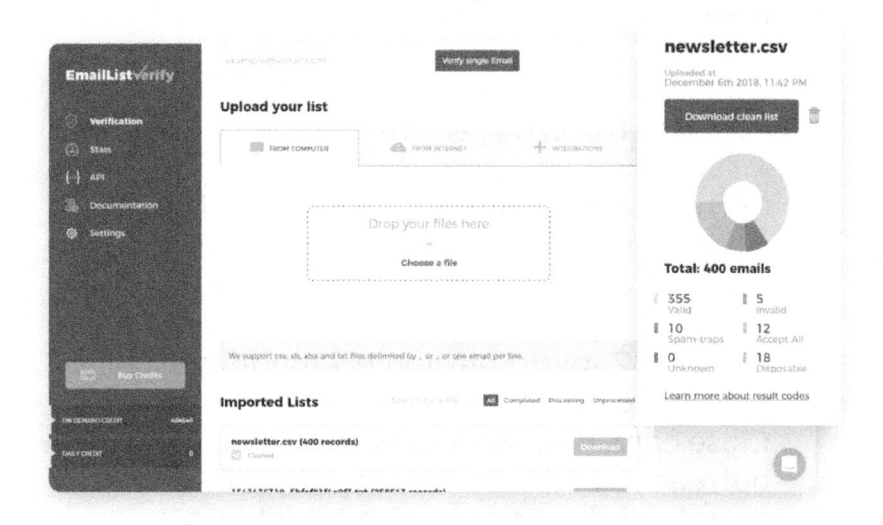

Voila Norbert

Rating: Beginner
Features:
- Bulk email list verification
- Customizable with different programming languages
- B2B email addresses

Voila Norbert eliminates the uncertainty of finding the right email addresses. While there are many email finding tools available, Voila

Norbert stands out with its vast array of integrations and upgrades. It is designed to accommodate teams of any size, making it a scalable solution.

You can kick-start your experience with 50 free leads and then upgrade to a $49 monthly plan for unlimited team access. Voila Norbert boasts a remarkable success rate of up to 98 percent, and each search result comes with a confidence rating to let you know how accurate the email address is.

Getting started with the API is effortless, and it works with popular programming languages such as Node.js, PHP, Python, and Ruby. The prospecting tool integrates with Google Chrome, Zapier, Salesforce, Pipedrive, Mailshake, Drip, ReplyApp, HubSpot, and Close.com, making it easy to streamline your outreach processes. The email verification tool seamlessly integrates with Mailchimp, SendGrid, Jotform, and Formstack, ensuring the accuracy of your email lists.

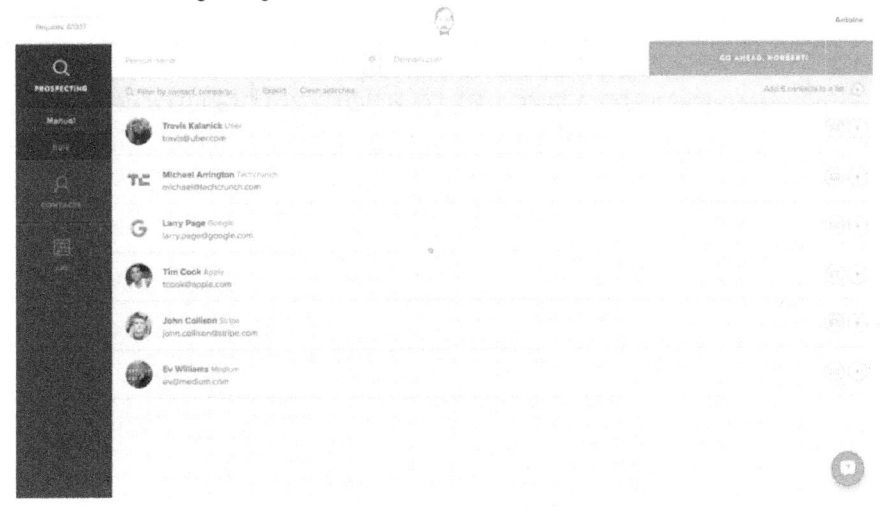

Email Deliverability Tools:

Mail-Tester
Rating: Beginner
Features:
- Tests your email deliverability
- Very simple to use
- Free to use

This is a free tool that analyzes your email scores. It's a less advanced version that allows you to send up to three email messages per day for free. You just go to their website and copy the email address generated for you, then you send your email to this address and receive a report.

You will receive a score (0-10) with 10 being the best. If you receive a score of five or six, you should probably invest in an email deliverability tool. This is great for independent recruiters or sourcers who don't have a large budget to address this problem. You can take this information and invest later down the line.

Spam Check from Postmark
Rating: Beginner
Features:
- Tests your email deliverability
- Fairly basic option on the market

This is another free tool to check your overall email deliverability. This tool will give you a basic score for you to help analyze what's happening with your emails. What's important to note is that the lower score you get here, the better. Anything close to five or higher will most likely automatically be marked as spam by your prospects' email providers.

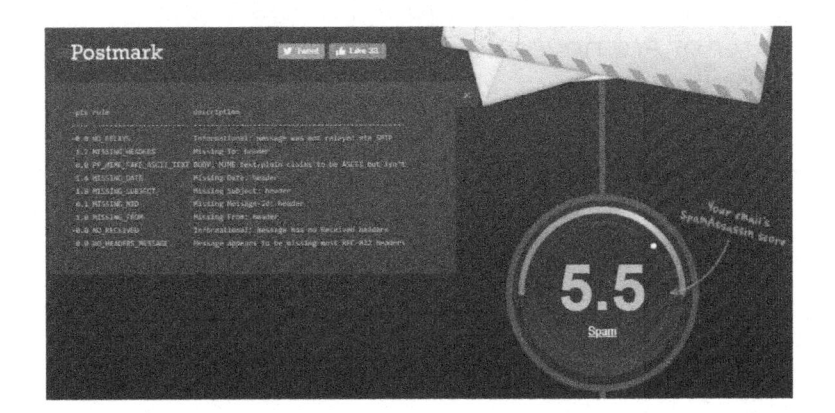

GlockApps

Rating: Advanced
Features:
- Tests your email deliverability
- Bulk testing features

If you are on a mid-to-large-scale recruiting team, it makes sense to invest in a well-developed tool that can cover all your bases. This tool has several advanced features that cover: inbox checkers, reputation checks, bounce analytics, template editors and overall content analysis. I would recommend getting a demo of this tool to see and understand all its benefits.

On average, 51 percent of emails never reach the inbox. So where do they go? Twenty-six percent go to spam or junk folders and 25 percent are never delivered. And the most common reasons are:

- Domain Reputation
- Authorization Fails
- IP Blacklisted
- Risky Content

Mailgun
Rating: Advanced
Features:

- Tests your email deliverability
- For large-scale recruiting teams

I was recommended this tool by my developer friend. This tool is more advanced and would be used to support a small recruiting agency with their email needs. Your deliverability is affected by a multitude of factors such as your industry, sending volume, traffic segmentation, and sender reputation. It makes sense to invest in a

100

large-scale tool if you have a team of recruiters that rely heavily on email outreach.

When you sign up for an account, you will be assigned an account manager. They will assess the current state of your email strategy and infrastructure and advise you on how to build out a deliverability strategy custom to your business.

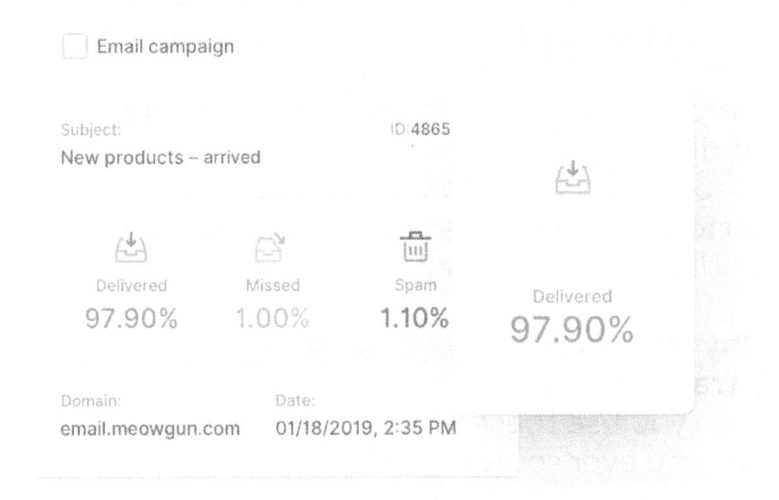

Email campaign			
Subject: New products – arrived			ID: 4865
Delivered 97.90%	Missed 1.00%	Spam 1.10%	Delivered 97.90%
Domain: email.meowgun.com		Date: 01/18/2019, 2:35 PM	

Here's what Mailgun Offers:
- Deliverability and recipient engagement management.
- Managed IP warmup ensures the health of your IP.
- Email tracking and testing consulting.
- Email reputation and deliverability reports.

Chapter 6: Web Scraping and Extraction Tools

As a Sourcer, I rely on various tools to gather valuable information on potential candidates. One of my top resources is web scraping and data extraction tools, which enable me to gather information from any web page with ease.

Web scraping tools automate the process of collecting data from websites, saving time and effort. This makes it an indispensable tool for Sourcers who are on the hunt for the right candidate to fill their role. With a range of web scraping tools available, I have handpicked the top four options to help you streamline your candidate sourcing process.

Why Do You Need Web Scraping and Extraction Tools?
Once you use these tools, you will wonder how you ever sourced without them. The amount of additional information you get is amazing, and the tools being created are getting increasingly more effective.

Whether you are just beginning with scraping or have been doing it for a while, these tools can help you take your sourcing game to the next level.

OutWit Hub
Rating: Beginner
Features:
- Desktop tool
- Recruiting SEO analysis
- Export data in CSV, HTML, Excel file
- Web and social media data collecting

OutWit Hub explores the depths of the web for you, automatically collecting and organizing data and media from online sources. OutWit Hub breaks down web pages into their different components. Navigating from page to page automatically, it extracts information elements and organizes them into usable collections.

With simple intuitive features as well as sophisticated scraping functions and data structure recognition, the program covers a broad range of needs. Though OutWit's automated scraping seems designed to meet somewhat advanced users with specific extraction needs, the design of the application makes it accessible to anyone. In a single click in the side panel, you change the view and see the extracted data, document, or images.

The contents extracted from a web page are presented in an easy and visual way, without requiring any programming skills or advanced technical knowledge. Users can easily extract links, images, email addresses, RSS news, data tables, and more from series of pages without ever seeing the source code. Extracted data can be exported to CSV, HTML, Excel or SQL databases, while images and documents are directly saved to your hard disk.

Also, there are other features you can use, like SEO analytics, advertising, deep web researching, e-commerce, images and more. Making an account and using this tool for web scraping is free and you can download your desired data with just one click of the download button.

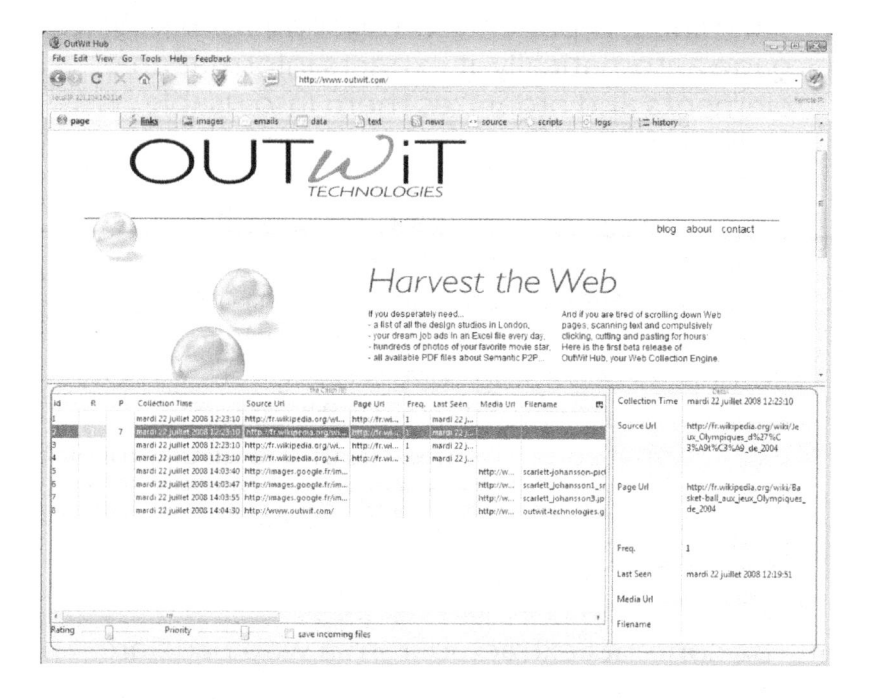

Data Scraper
Rating: Beginner

Features:
- AI-based researching
- Precise results
- Use on small and large websites

Data Scraper extracts data from web pages and exports it as Excel or CSV files. This is an automated data extraction tool for any website. It uses AI to predict which data is most relevant on a HTML page and allows you to save it to an Excel or CSV file (XLS, XLSX, and CSV).

This tool does not require website specific scripts, instead it uses heuristic AI analysis of HTML structure to detect data for extraction. If the prediction is not satisfactory, it lets the user customize the selections for greater accuracy. This type of scraping technology is much more convenient because it does not require large user created libraries of scraping scripts, which often become filled with outdated and redundant versions.

That means that this scraping method works just as well with small and lesser known websites as it does with global giants like Amazon. Also, the users do not need to have any coding, JSON or XML skills, which is a big benefit.

Data Scraper Features Include:
- Detecting data for extraction with AI.
- Detecting when dynamic data has loaded.

- Delay and maximum wait time customization for desired crawling speed
- Support for pagination on websites.
- Automatic navigation to next page via buttons or links.
- Support for infinite scrolling.
- Extracted data preview with copy and paste support.
- Data export to Excel spreadsheet or CSV file.
- Extracted data column renaming and filtering.

This tool uses Xpath, JQuery, and CSS selector to identify the information in the HTML web page. Then it scrapes that information and presents it to you in the form of a table which you can save as a CSV or XLS file and open it in spreadsheets. Fill form works similarly but inserts the data as well.

Data Scraper is a data converter, extractor, and crawler combined into one which can harvest emails or any other text from web pages. It supports UTF-8, so it scrapes Chinese, Japanese, Russian, and many other languages with ease. You do not need to have coding, XML, or JSON experience.

Dux-Soup
Rating: Advanced
Features:
- Best option for LinkedIn scraping

- Visit or scan profiles for leads
- Great for building a network
- Offers a free trial

If LinkedIn is primarily where you want to focus your scraping efforts, the best option will be Dux-Soup. It is the top tool used for the social networking platform and for a good reason. This is the only option of the three which isn't free, but it offers a free trial so you can test it out before committing.

With Dux-Soup, you can visit or scan profiles to build your network and create leads. Visiting profiles will get you more data, like degrees and full work history, while scanning is faster but gives only the basic information. Dux-Soup's Medium page provides a full breakdown of the difference between visiting and scanning profiles and suggests you think about your goal to help determine which method to use.

After your free trial, you will need to decide whether to go with the starter or pro-option. The starter option is free but has limited access to the tools you need to get the most out of the tool. I recommend using the Starter version until you feel comfortable, then upgrading to Pro. At $15 a month, it's not too pricey and definitely worth the upgrade.

Instant Data Scraper
Rating: Beginner

Features:
- No-brainer if you use Chrome
- Free and easy to use
- Simple enough for beginners
- Extract data to Excel

If you like to use Chrome already, this option is a no-brainer. Instant Data Scraper is a Chrome extension that is free and easy to use. This extension is simple enough for even beginners to grasp. Another great feature is that the extension allows you to extract the data straight into Excel.

While it's great for extracting simple pages, it's not ideal for more complex sites. If you are looking for a simple extraction, this is probably your best option. To download the extension, you can go to the Chrome store. This is probably the easiest option for beginners to get the hang of data scraping before moving on to more complex scraping.

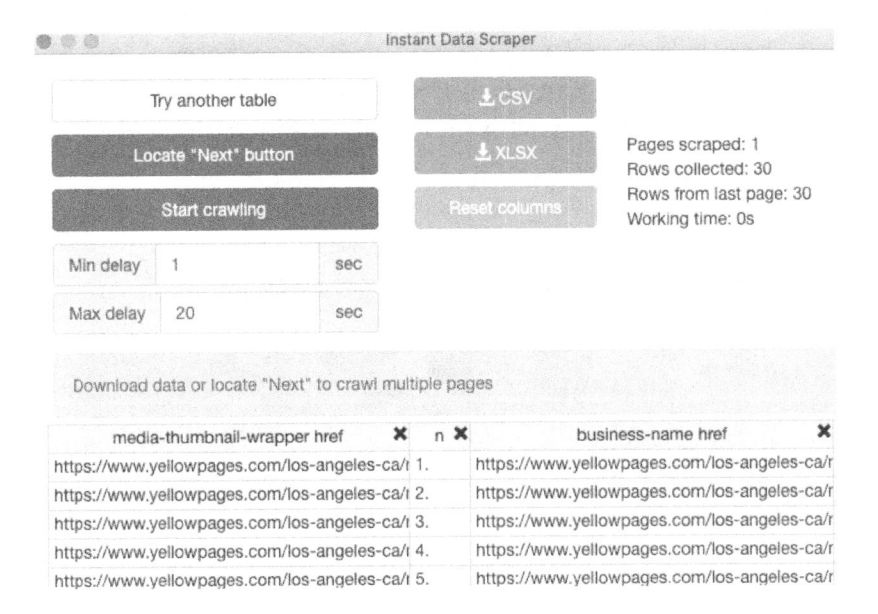

Data Miner + Recipe Creator
Rating: Beginner
Features:
- Two-in-one tool
- Export to Excel or CSV file
- Use it alongside Recipe Creator

This option is like having two tools in one. Similar to the previous option, Data Miner is a free Chrome extension that exports data from websites to an Excel or a CSV file. To make Data Miner even better, use it along with another free Chrome extension called Recipe Creator. This creates "recipes" to tell it what data you want.

Don't worry if you don't have experience with this thing; the Recipe Creator walks you through step by step, making it easy to understand and use. There are also communities and a Live Support function to help if you get stuck.

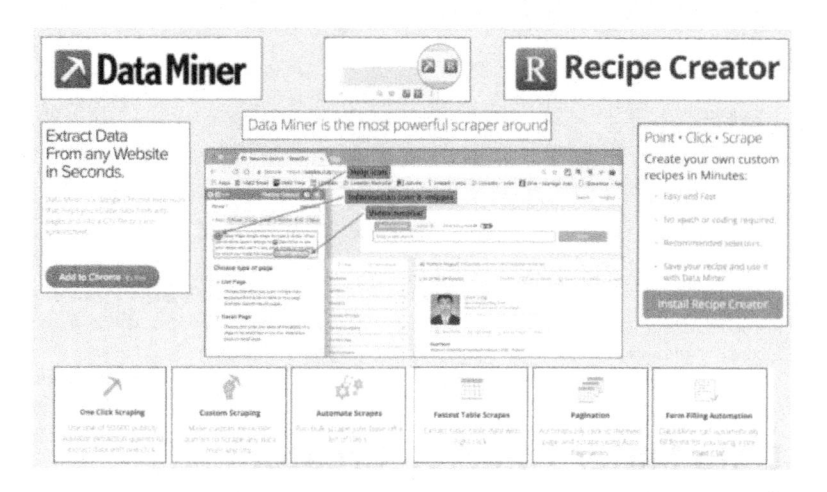

Web Scraper
Rating: Beginner
Features:
- Build sitemaps to easily extract data
- Scrape text, tables, images, and more
- Export data into a CSV file

Using Web Scraper, you can build sitemaps that will navigate the site and extract the data. Using different type selectors, the Web Scraper will navigate the site and extract multiple types of data – text, tables, images, links and more.

After you've scraped the data, you can easily export it into a CSV file. Overall, it's fairly easy

110

to use and comes highly recommended by the sourcing community.

Web Scraper can extract data from sites with multiple levels of navigation. It can navigate a website on all levels.

- Categories and subcategories
- Pagination
- Product pages

Web Scraper allows you to build Site Maps from different types of selectors. This system makes it possible to tailor data extraction to different site structures. Build scrapers, scrape sites and export data in CSV format directly from your browser. Use Web Scraper Cloud to export data in CSV, XLSX and JSON formats, access it via API, webhooks, or export it via Dropbox. This is an awesome feature because you can use the cloud systems to import and export your data.

Web Scraper utilizes a modular structure that is made of selectors, which instructs the scraper on how to traverse the target site and what data to extract. Thanks to this structure, Web Scraper is able to extract information from modern and dynamic websites such as Amazon, TripAdvisor, eBay, and so on, as well as from smaller, lesser-known websites.

Note: this is a paid tool, but you can use it for free as a Chrome extension.

The first paid Project package gives you 5000 credits for $50 per month. Next, is the Professional package, where the users can get up to 20,000 cloud credits for $100 per month.

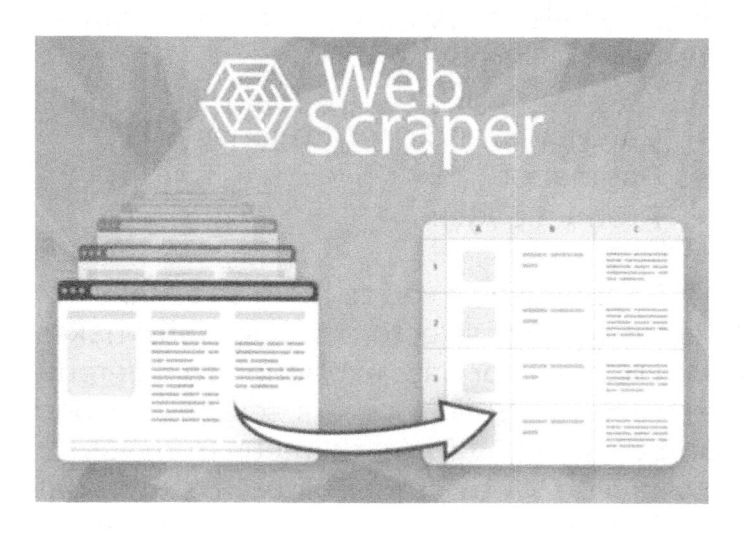

Chapter 7: Automation Tools

Recruitment automation is a set of automated processes, actions, and sequences designed to streamline your recruitment tasks. These tools can save you a significant amount of time and effort when it comes to searching for talent, sourcing candidates, reaching out, and scheduling emails.

The adoption of recruitment automation by companies and HR teams has been rapidly increasing. Talent sourcing requires a lot of manual work such as searching, outreach, follow-up, scheduling, and many other tasks. A large part of my job involves data entry and guiding applicants through our process, which includes repetitive and time-consuming tasks that could be easily automated with technology.

There Are Four Levels of Automation in Recruiting:
Shally Steckerl has defined the four levels of Automation. The fourth is intelligent automation which would completely automate recruiting and sourcing with the use of AI. We might get to that level within our lifetime, but I doubt we'll get there within the next decade.

Basic Automation: Simple tasks, no special knowledge needed.

Process Automation: More complex – such as Microsoft 365 or Chatbots.

Integration Automation: Most difficult in-house, some human intervention (IFTTT).

Intelligent Automation: (AI) Advanced Robots doing multiple steps, no humans.

Why Do You Need Automation Tools?
As a recruiter, you have multiple responsibilities that include posting jobs, interviewing, prioritizing daily tasks, and understanding your clients' needs or hiring managers to locate and recruit the best talent for the job.

Of course, some of these tasks require your full attention and hands on involvement, but there are automation tools that can help streamline repetitive tasks and save you time.

Machine Sourcer
Rating: Intermediate
Features:
- LinkedIn automation – automatically view profiles and send messages.
- Create projects, auto send connections or InMail messages
- It will save you time and effort while building a LinkedIn network

Machine Sourcer is a great tool if you want to expand your network fast. You can use this tool on all of LinkedIn except Sales Recruiter and LinkedIn Recruiter.

This tool will save you time by quickly growing your professional network on LinkedIn using many advanced search filters, automated connecting and messaging, and you can do this all while you are away from your computer.

Machine Sourcer is the more affordable, easier to use, and more powerful alternative to Linked Helper. Here is what you need to do to start using this amazing Chrome extension:

1. Install the extension using the Chrome store
2. Register and verify your Email
3. Go to LinkedIn and open the Machine Sourcer Extension
4. Enter your search criteria
5. Start connecting and messaging
6. Enable the extension and open LinkedIn. The enable extension is the puzzle symbol on the top right of your browser where your extensions sit.

115

Linked Helper II

Rating: Advanced
Features:

- Auto view LinkedIn profiles
- Send automated connection request and follow-up messages
- CRM capabilities

It is obvious that Linked Helper is the most powerful LinkedIn automation software. When using it you can automatically invite targeted second and third level contacts with a personal note. There are different features such as:

1. **Build smart message chains:** Auto-responder to newly added connections and drip campaigns for chain messaging with reply detection

2. **LinkedIn lead generation on steroids:** Dozens of features and tools for LinkedIn, Sales Navigator and Recruiter automation
3. **Save contacts to built-in CRM or export into CSV file:** Manage your LinkedIn connections and lead funnel with a convenient CRM system

What LinkedIn Helper offers:

Profiles Auto-visitor: You can auto view profiles based on your search string. There used to be about half a dozen tools that did a similar thing. If you do not pay for a premium account on LinkedIn, I wouldn't recommend using this feature because you probably will get sent to LinkedIn jail.

Auto Connecting: Easily expand your network. This allows you to connect with an unlimited amount of profiles. Again, I would only target your niche and use this with caution.

Inmail Signature: When you do connect and auto-sending a message. This allows you to include your signature in the message footer. This is a great way to communicate your contact information and it will help cut down on mundane tasks.

Automating Inmails: This system allows you to automatically send out pre-created inmails to your 1st connections.

Autoresponder to New Connections: Send messages to recently added connections. You could automatically create an introduction message. Have your leads feel important and connected into your network right away.

Group Messaging: Send messages to LinkedIn Group Members. Find your niche and create a targeted inmail that grabs their attention.

Group Invites: Invite 1st connections to join a LinkedIn Group. Easily build a niche and create a network community group.

Easily Build a List: Export your LinkedIn contacts to CSV file and build targeted emailing list.

Automating Endorsements: Boost your profile and get hundreds of endorsements from other users. Automatically sends endorsements to all your contacts. These endorsement keywords will help boost your profile in search results.

This LinkedIn tool is a top-rated application with 5-star ratings and 90,000+ users. Also, it will help you to make your LinkedIn account safer. Linked Helper remains the safest tool for LinkedIn automation as it is a web browser that does not embed its code into LinkedIn page. It does not call LinkedIn API unlike most cloud-based tools. This tool is not a Chrome extension, so you can use it only as a type of web browser.

Linked Helper is a paid tool, but you can activate a free trial for 14 days.

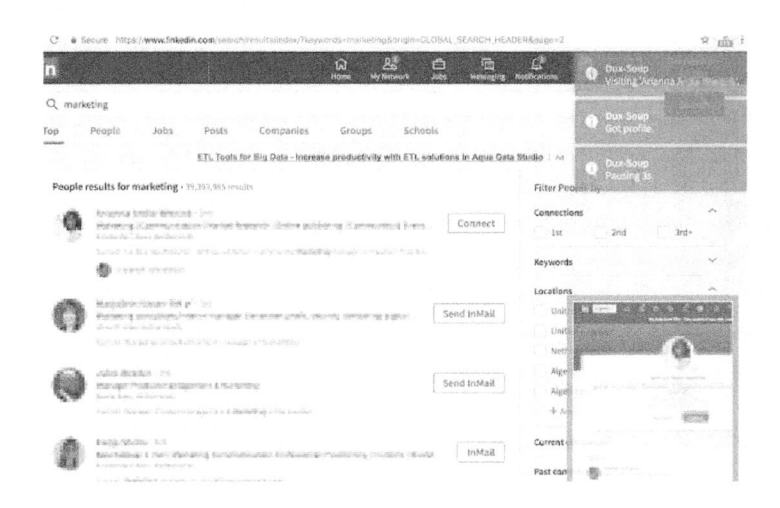

SourceWhale

Rating: Advanced
Features:
- Send InMail and email messages within the extension
- Create email drip campaigns – four-to-five sequences

SourceWhale replaces all the sourcing tools you currently use, delivers personalized automated outreach and follow-ups, and provides detailed analytics throughout your recruiting process.

Dashboard
Create campaign sequences, track click rates, diversity metrics, and CRM notes all within one place.

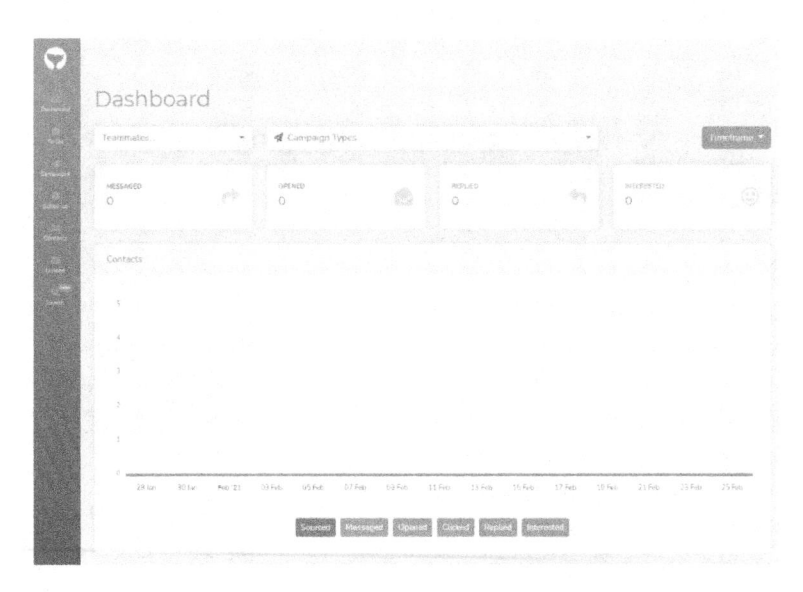

The tool also has a Boolean Generator tab

External Extension
Use on LinkedIn, Stack Overflow, GitHub, and many others to create an email campaign sequence. From the extension the tool helps

find email and cell phone information. You can also choose and edit a template campaign.

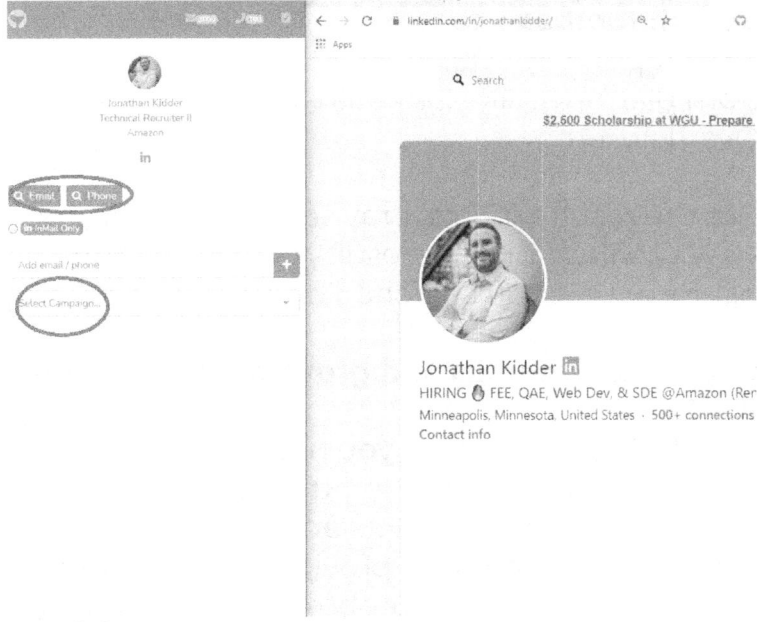

Webbtree
Rating: Advanced
Features:
- Send InMail and email messages within the extension
- Fully automate your outreaches within the tool

Webbtree is a free recruiting SaaS solution with the goal of empowering recruiters to source talent more efficiently in this digital age. This CRM solution enables you to find, enrich, and nurture talent from across the public web. This tool has many different features that include:

contacting finding, message automation, and tracking CRM leads.

Search toolbox
Search publicly available candidate profiles from platforms like LinkedIn, GitHub, Stack Overflow, etc.

Get the results of this x-ray search in Webbtree, view profiles from the results on the specific platform that you searched on.

Get contact details and grow talent pools on the fly
Enrich the profiles that you have sourced, with contact related data. Webbtree looks for publicly available contacts and social profile links of candidates and provides them to you for free. Additionally, Webbtree allows you to look for contacts from premium sources.

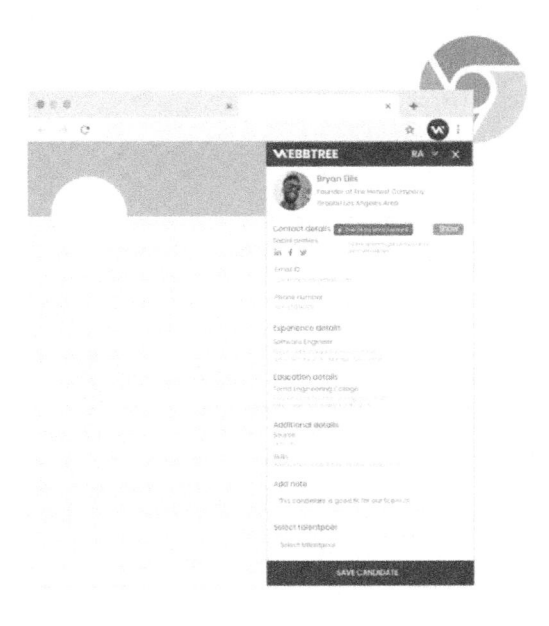

From source to nurture in 15 seconds

Create personalized email campaigns to engage candidates at scale. All replies to these emails will be sent to your registered email ID. Track all the emails sent through Webbtree against a candidate profile.

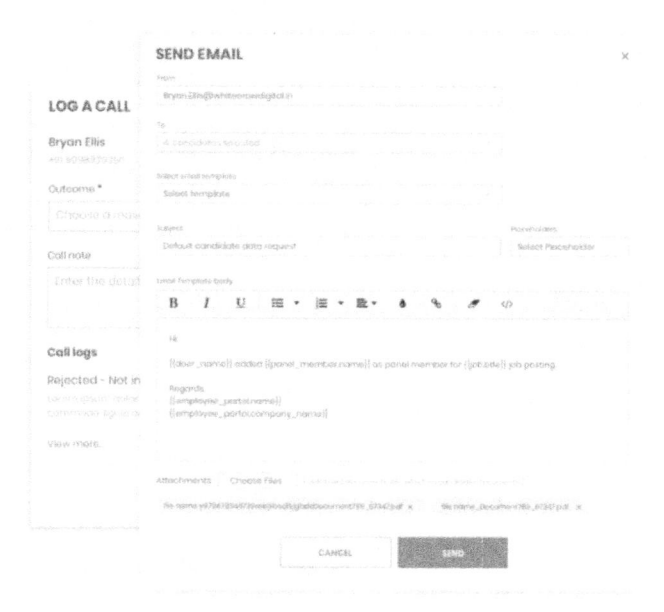

Talent pipeline
Get rid of spreadsheets. Perform CRM and track candidates on a simple cloud-based platform. Group candidates into different lists. If you wish to share candidates, download these lists as an Excel sheet.

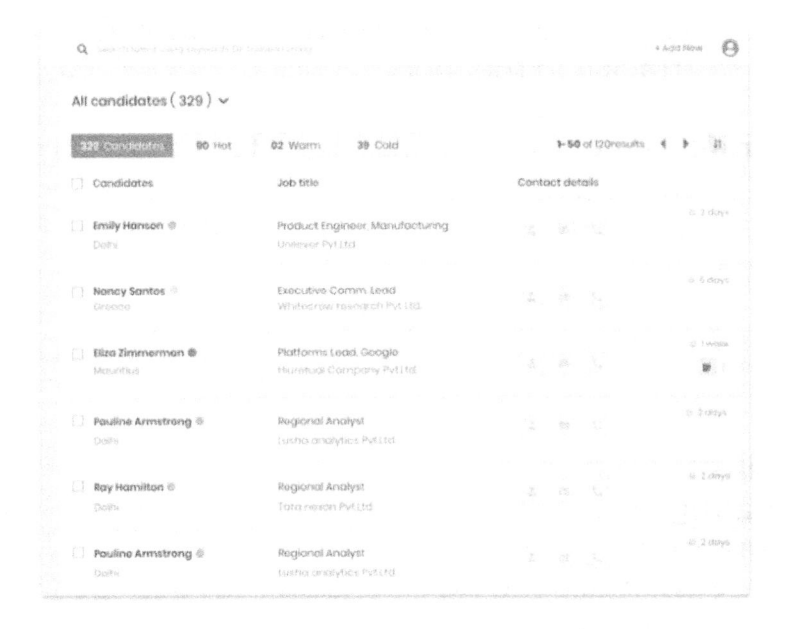

Additional Features include:
- X-ray search for candidates from multiple websites in one platform.
- Access LinkedIn profiles that are out of your third-degree network.
- Search for technical candidates across Stack Overflow, GitHub and AngelList.
- Enrich contact information for profiles you find across the web.
- Use the Chrome extension to easily grab profiles into a single format from across the web and add them to your talent pipeline
- Say goodbye to Excel sheets. Now track all your candidate relationships in talent pipelines to add more meaning to your interaction.

- Send emails to the sourced talent and track it in the tool.

Professional Account ($39 per Month - 2022)
- 10 JD parsing
- Unlimited Basic contact enrichments
- 50 Contact enrichments
- 500 Smart emails
- 10 Talent pipelines

Hireflow.ai
Rating: Advanced
Features:
- Contact finding extension with outreach automation features
- AI automation searching features
- Diversity searching capabilities

Hireflow.ai is a new all-in-one AI-recruiting platform that helps source and engage candidates online. The tool was recently launched within the Chrome store and I was lucky to get a quick demo from Eda Topuz. At its core, Hireflow is an AI-automation tool that helps find contact information on potential leads and then it auto generates an email template message for outreach. You can easily track response rates and clicks within the tool. Overall, it's got great potential and can be used to source candidates more efficiently within LinkedIn.

Advanced Search AI Sourcing
- The tool learns your requirements and suggests more leads.
- Approve and rank profiles before you send any outreach.
- Continually learns from your feedback and improves on the search.
- Discovers the hard-to-find candidates that are missing brand name pedigree.
- Get your daily sourcing done within 5-10 minutes – 10x faster.
- Get 50 qualified leads per week – This is an enterprise level feature.

Email Outreach Campaigns
- One click sourcing with the Chrome extension.
- Automated email follow-ups, personalization, response rate optimization, inbox integration, and email lookups.
- The tool also integrates with many ATS/CRM tools.
- Source 3x faster and stay in your flow.

CRM Tracking

- Powerful data and analytics to help you focus on the right candidates.
- Collaborate with your team to keep track of candidates.
- Double response rates with nurture campaign follow-ups.
- Re-engage prospects that showed interest in your email outreach but did not respond.
- Emails are optimized to send at the right time of day.

Track Diversity Efforts

Draft and Send Messages via the Extension

Use the extension to auto populate messages based on a user's LinkedIn summary information. Use the tools to send the outreach over email and track the results within the dashboard.

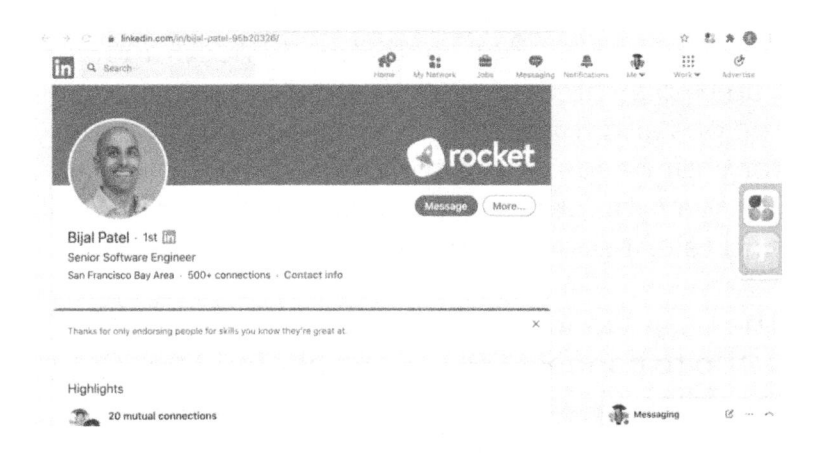

Marketing Automation Tools:

IFTTT
Rating: Beginner

Features:
- Easy-to-use automation tool
- Connects with all sorts of apps
- Create your own "recipes" to reduce your workload

IFTTT (If This Then That) is an ideal tool for email automation. It has features that allow you to create reminders for yourself, handle repetitive tasks, and formulate specific triggers. It's a free, web-based service to create chains of simple conditional statements, called applets or recipes.

You can use these recipes to automate different recruitment activities. I encourage you to play around with these different recipes and figure out which ones work best for your needs. These tools will truly impact the way you automate certain recruitment and talent sourcing duties.

The user-friendly application requires a brief setup to connect the various platforms used including LinkedIn, Dropbox, Google calendar, and Facebook, to program the desired actions.

Some useful actions might include sending an email to yourself when new jobs are posted on LinkedIn or Craigslist; programming your phone to automatically text you, providing an escape for those times when an interviewee has exceeded their block of time, and you can't get away.

Recipe Recommendations for Recruiting:
1. New LinkedIn contacts in a Google Drive Spreadsheet
2. Send new contacts a "Nice to meet you!" email
3. Save contacts added to a Google Contacts group as a subscriber to a list in Mailchimp
4. Save caller's contact information each time I receive a call
5. Create a calendar item to follow-up in a week when a new contact is added

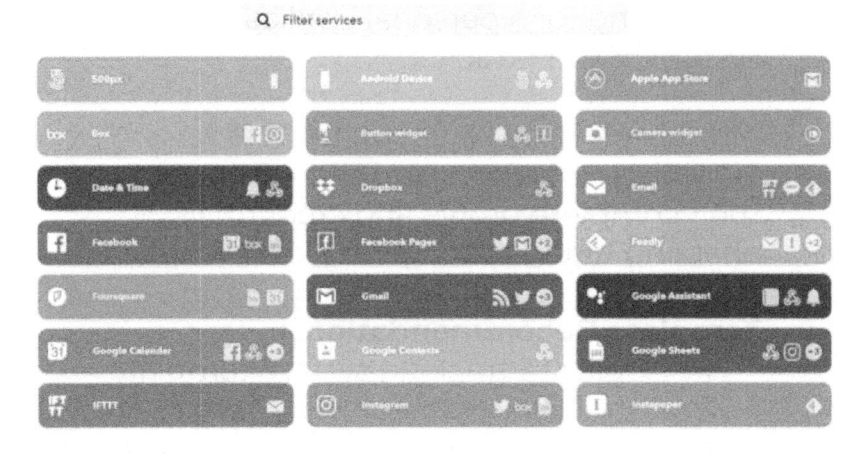

Airtable
Rating: Intermediate
Features:
- Easily link related data records

- Use Blocks to visualize and summarize
- Utilize pre-built templates
- Create your own templates and integrate with other tools
- Easily create a sales tracker, sourcing funnel, or ATS/CRM system

Airtable combines the best features of database applications and spreadsheets into a single hybrid application that allows you to compile information, sort data, link items together, and share the information with others as well as publish details on websites.

Its ability to integrate with applications such as Zapier makes it possible for recruiters to track candidates and share pertinent information via email. It's a great option if you are looking for a personal application tracking system or CRM tracker.

Airtable can also be set up to include candidate overviews and shareable links to their complete profile and credentials, enabling hiring managers to review specifics.

Template Recommendations:
1. Applicant tracking system template
2. Employee onboarding template
3. University recruiting or job fair event list template
4. Competitor tracking template
5. Email marketing campaign template

Zapier

Rating: Intermediate
Features:
- Integrate multiple web apps
- Create custom automations
- Connect and integrate with over 1,500 platforms

Zapier is an application that makes it possible to integrate various other web-based apps as a way to customize the automation. Zapier can communicate with other platforms, including Office 365, Google Calendar, Google Docs, Gmail, QuickBooks, Trello, Airtable, Slack, and LinkedIn. Through the use of Zapier, you can share information between multiple apps automatically versus repeat manual entry.

Zapier can help streamline the process of sorting and selecting candidates based on criteria, so you have more time to focus on evaluating information or actually connecting with candidates.

I discovered Zapier a few months ago and I've been hooked ever since! It's similar to the website IFTTT where I've been experimenting with recipes for many years now. However, Zapier is a way better automation tool in comparison. Zapier is the glue that connects over 1,500+ web apps. These apps connect to trigger an event.

You can use these pre-built zaps to automate mundane recruitment tasks. These apps can help with Calendar Scheduling, Call Tracking, Contacts, CRM, Emailing, Management tools, Human Resource tools — and the lists goes on! There are endless opportunities to use these apps in recruitment.

Zapier App Recommendations:
- Create Google Calendar events (quick add events) from Evernote reminders.
- Update rows on Google Sheets when someone new cancels on Calendly.
- Create Google Sheets rows from scheduled Calendly events.
- Create a call log or meeting note in Streak when a Calendly event is created.
- Send emails to lost Myphoner leads via Gmail.
- Send emails to new Myphoner winners via Gmail.

- Enrich company names in Google Sheets with data from Clearbit.
- Add person and company data from Clearbit to new Mailchimp subscribers.
- Search Clearbit and save the results to Evernote via a Google Chrome extension.
- Enrich contacts in Google Sheets with emails and phone numbers using Lusha.
- Enrich new contacts on HubSpot CRM with enhanced personal contact details via Lusha.
- Create or update HubSpot CRM contacts from new Google Contacts.
- Create Streak boxes for new Google Contacts.
- Create boxes in Streak from new updated rows in Google Sheets.
- Save new Gmail attachments (original file format) to Google Drive.
- Look up a Google Sheet row and find and edit a box in Streak from new Gmail threads.
- Create a Mailchimp Mailing List for Job Applicants.
- Import Job Candidates from Gmail into Workable by Labeling Emails.
- Create Workable candidates from a Google Sheets spreadsheet.

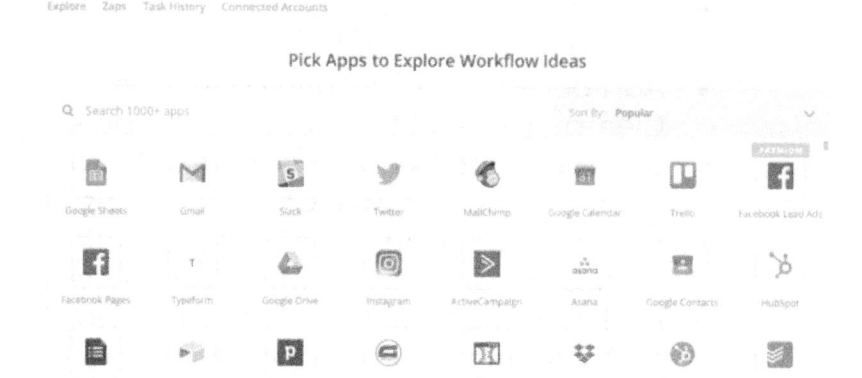

Phantombuster

Rating: Intermediate

Features:
- Extract data from platforms
- Profile scraper, social media scheduler, auto responder and much more
- Automate repetitive tasks with talent sourcing
- Combine with AI to save more time

Phantombuster is used to extract data from platforms that can be used to automate necessary but repetitive tasks in recruiting. Phantombuster can be programmed to search certain profile data or URLs across networks such as Instagram, LinkedIn, Facebook, and Twitter, which can be compiled into a spreadsheet or CRM for review. The collected data can also help generate leads, be used to update network profiles, and be shared with others.

AI and other automation tools have definitely been on the rise lately. It's an exciting time to be in the talent sourcing world because we can use these same cutting-edge innovation tools to source, research, and automate certain recruitment tasks.

It was created to help marketers use different API's to automate and boost different marketing efforts. You can use one API tool for 10 minutes a day for free. I recommend testing out several tools before you decide to pay for the upgraded growth hacker account, which is $29 per month.

Tool Recommendations:
- Facebook Profile URL Finder
- Instagram Profile URL Finder
- LinkedIn Profile Scraper
- Twitter Profile URL Finder
- LinkedIn Accept Invitations
- LinkedIn Network Booster
- LinkedIn Search Export
- LinkedIn Auto-Follow/Accept

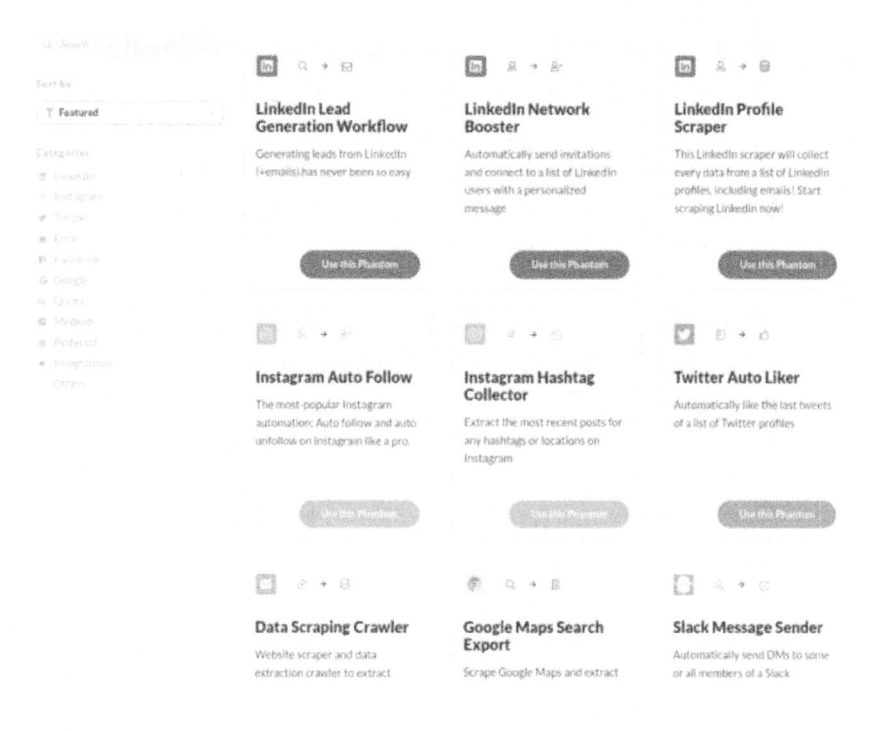

Microsoft Flow

Rating: Advanced
Features:

- Simplify automation between services and application
- Add and copy files across platforms
- Automate your push notifications
- Collect information across platforms

Microsoft Flow simplifies the automation process between services and applications. It can be used to simultaneously add and copy files between multiple platforms, automate push notifications, or collect information from multiple platforms based on identified triggers.

For example, rather than checking email throughout the day to check for candidate responses or messages from clients, you can set up Microsoft Flow to notify and automatically forward applicable messages to you.

This tool has amazing features, such as:

1. Boost productivity - Build time-saving workflows into everything from individual tasks to large-scale systems with seamless integration using hundreds of pre-built connectors.

2. Automate quickly and more securely - Enable everyone to build secure workflows with a low-code, no-code guided experience to automate mundane everyday tasks with robotic process automation (RPA).

3. Put intelligent workflows to work - Automate time-consuming manual tasks with built-in AI capabilities, giving you more time to focus on strategic, high-value opportunities.

Keep in mind that Microsoft Flow is a paid tool, but you can start a free trial for a couple of days. For $15 per month, you will be allowed to invite individual users to create unlimited flows based on their unique needs. For $40 per month, you will get 5,000 AI Builder service credits for the whole month and a bunch of other amazing features. Lastly, $500 per month with unlimited features.

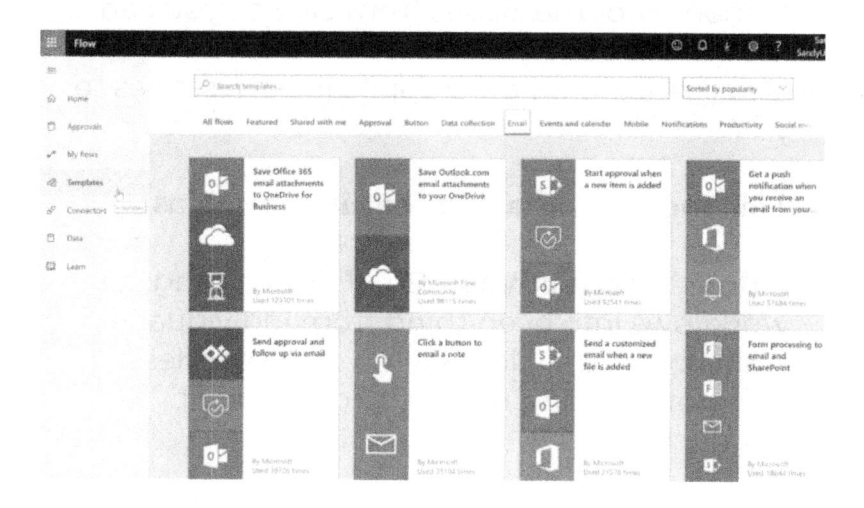

Clay
Rating: Advanced
Features:
- Connect all your apps to one platform
- Tons of automation templates

Clay is a cutting-edge tool for recruiters that streamlines, automates and integrates the recruitment process. Utilize data from various sources and uncover new prospecting opportunities with access to over 50 data sources such as live LinkedIn data, automated Google searches, website keyword searches, technology stack analysis, job posting scraping and personalized emails generated by GPT-3. Find potential leads with ease and efficiency. Sandra Feldmann has been advocating for ChatGPT and Clay integrations for some time and she suggested that I evaluate this new tool, and I am happy she did!

How can recruiters benefit from using clay?
Clay is a platform that helps recruiters automate and streamline their recruitment processes. It offers a range of tools and features that allow recruiters to:

1. Source and engage with potential candidates
2. Track and manage the candidate pipeline
3. Schedule and conduct virtual interviews
4. Collaborate with team members and stakeholders
5. Monitor recruitment metrics and performance

By using Clay, recruiters can save time and effort on manual tasks, improve the efficiency of their recruitment processes, and make data-driven decisions. Ultimately, this can lead to better candidate experiences, higher quality hires, and a more successful recruitment outcome.

Workato
Rating: Intermediate
Features:
- Connect all your apps to one platform
- Drag-and-drop interface

- Create triggers to automate an action

Workato is an automation app that allows you to connect a variety of apps within a single platform. Using the easy drag-and-drop functions, you simply choose a combination of apps and create triggers to complete an action.

As a recruiter, that action may be notifying you of an event such as the acceptance of a contract or candidate application or alerting you to a receipt of an important message on Slack or email.

Their slogan is with great power comes great simplicity, so the features include:

1. Enterprise Power
- Enterprise iPaaS leader
- Offers AI, bots and more
- Intelligent data loss prevention

2. Serverless Operation
- Elastic Scaling
- Built-in redundancy
- No Dev Ops required

3. Maximum Security
- Industry-leading security and governance
- Trusted by the largest financial institutions

4. Speed and Simplicity
- No coding required
- Automated error handling

- Instant deployment

To start using it, you just need to log in on their official site and start using it for free.

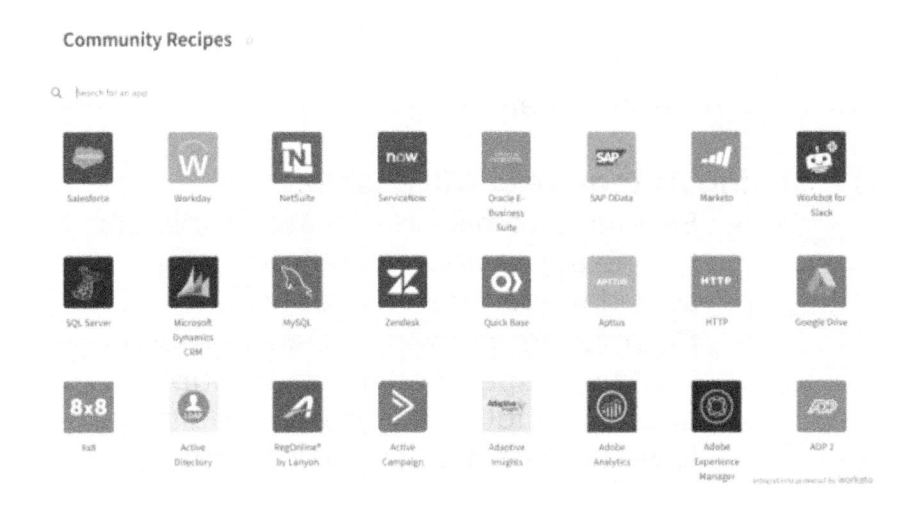

Automate.io
Rating: Beginner
Features:
- Connect a number of apps
- Automate your workflows
- Create chat bots
- Sync data across apps

This is a cloud application that connects with a variety of other apps that make it easy to automate workflows, program chat bots, or simply sync data between applications.

From tagging others in email to setting it up to notify you when a website application is completed which automatically notifies the candidate via email, and then compiles data according to conditional criteria and logic. Easily integrate with over 100 apps, including Typeform, Google, social media platforms, Salesforce, and more. Automate.io features a simple drag-and-drop interface making it user-friendly for anyone.

Using Automate.io will enable:
- Simple Automation - Create simple one-to-one automation workflows, or just sync data between two apps.
- Complex Workflows - Create complex workflows spanning across multiple apps in minutes. Add delay, conditional logic, and format data and do much more.

Here are the most popular features:
- **Simple and Intuitive**: Visually create integrations with drag-drop data mapping in minutes. No IT help required.
- **100+ Connectors:** Connectors for all leading cloud and SaaS applications available. Use the web hooks and rest API to connect other apps.
- **Powerful Tools:** Format data, add conditional logic or time delay into your workflows.
- **Secure and Reliable**: Data encryption at rest and transit, data retention controls and audit logs

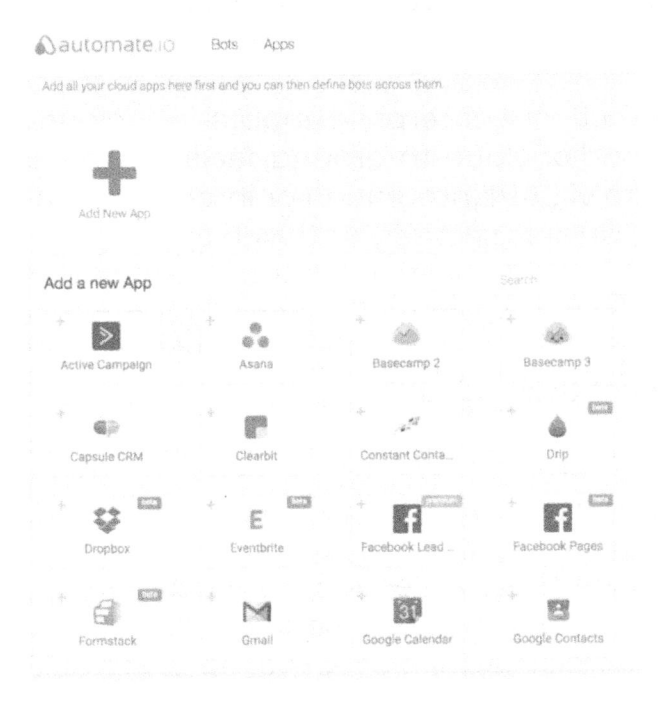

Elastic.io
Rating: Beginner
Features:
- Share data across applications
- Hybrid integration
- Cost-effective solution

Elastic.io is a cloud platform that makes it possible to share data between applications, SaaS systems, and multiple devices for quick, easy access. Its hybrid integration works with cloud-to-cloud platforms and just as easily with cloud-to-ground. The integration capabilities of Elastic.io offer a cost-effective solution for managing a variety of business processes.

Connect your enterprise applications cloud-to-cloud or cloud-to-ground, facilitate the flow of data via API integration or integrate with B2B partners securely and with ease. SaaS users want applications that play well within their own ecosystem. Enhance your product with out-of-the-box integration infrastructure to meet their needs.

It saves time and money immensely. We used to spend from 10-30 days building an average integration; now we need about 10-15 hours to integrate the pre-defined connectors. Keep in mind that Elastic.io is a paid tool, but you can start a free trial for a couple of days. For $199 per month, you will get basic connections and production workspaces.

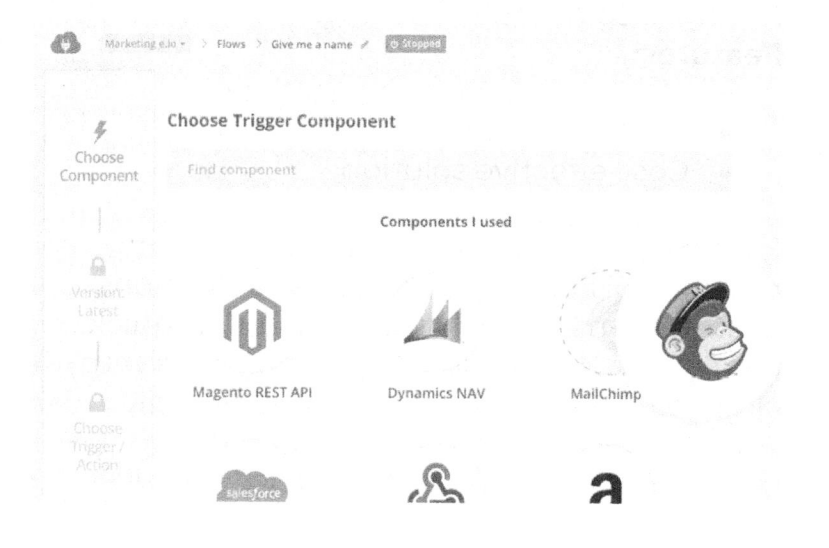

Blockspring
Rating: Beginner
Features:
- Similar to IFTTT, Phantombuster, and Zapier
- Connect APIs to automate tasks
- Great for non-technical users
- Great for creating sourcing trackers, sales trackers, and ATS/CRM systems

The tool is part of a sweeping effort to bring coding skills to a wider swath of the population. Blockspring is a series of coding API tools that can be used inside a spreadsheet either in Google Sheets or in Microsoft Excel. Users and companies have been creating new applications and you can use these as building blocks to conduct various tasks.

It's similar to Phantombuster, Zapier, IFTTT, and Airtable, which connect API's and automate certain tasks. Blockspring was founded by three entrepreneurs Kasten, Pinkus, and Tokoph and their goal was to turn a billion non-technical users into software engineers across the globe.

Do anything in a spreadsheet. Connect Google Sheets to hundreds of web apps and services to automate more of your work. Blockspring makes it simple to connect Google Sheets to hundreds of web apps and data services. Founders, digital marketers, sales teams, and recruiters use Blockspring to automate reporting, sales operations, sourcing, and much more.

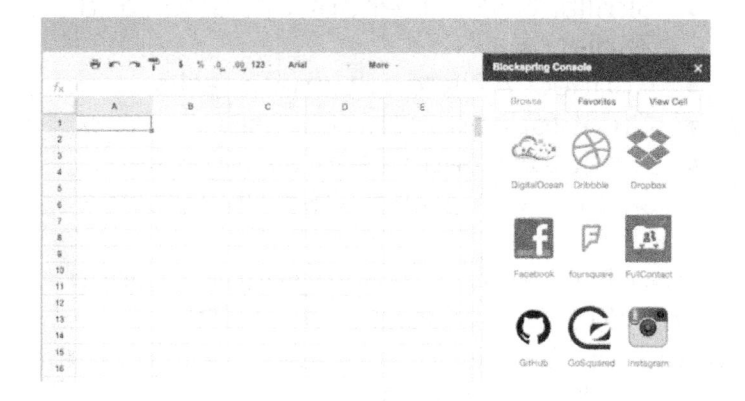

Chapter 8: Boolean Generators

Boolean string searches are powerful, but they can seem tricky. These tools help simplify and auto generate Boolean strings with ease.

Why Do You Need Boolean Generators?
As a Talent Sourcer, I'm constantly creating different Boolean strings for my searches. My day can easily get chaotic if I'm unorganized. I have hundreds of different search tabs open throughout the day. So, staying organized and having a place to store all my Boolean strings is important for my success.

(hireEZ) Hiretual "Boolean Generator"
Rating: Intermediate
Features:
- Use job descriptions or other skill-set requirements and it will auto create a string
- It has a large database of additional job title and search terms suggestions
- Have to pay to get access to this feature

Hiretual has a great internal Boolean generator within its platform. To begin your search, click on the Toolbox. From there, you can choose relevant job titles, skills, industry, and location and create Boolean search strings based on them. Then you can select any of the platforms on which to search.

They are divided into most popular, generic platforms: Tech, Healthcare, Designers, and Research, Mechanical, Games, and many more.

Select Search Talent Now, and your results will be visible in the next tab.

Recruitin.net
Rating: Beginner
Features:
- Simple user face
- Job title suggestions as you type
- Much faster loading

The tool gives you keywords that help your job ads rank in Google, Indeed, and job boards to ensure they resonate with candidates you're looking for. The more you use it, the better it gets. There's nothing else like it and it's still free and anonymous.

This tool is a simple way to construct the very same Boolean queries (and more), but with the benefit of a nice simple interface.

It's entirely free and anonymous and not in any way associated with LinkedIn, which is a registered trademark of the LinkedIn Corporation.

Recruit'em (formerly RecruitIn before LinkedIn's lawyers strenuously objected) is a project by Clever Biscuit, five professional computer types who build free tools to help people out. Also, this tool has awesome integration in different platforms, like:

- LinkedIn
- Dribble
- GitHub
- Xing
- Stack Overflow
- Twitter

BooleanAssistant
Rating: Beginner
Features:
- Has a large library of Boolean string examples
- Connect APIs to automate tasks
- Great for non-technical users

This Chrome extension is free to use and installing it is such a simple process. Just go on Google and type the BooleanAssistant. With one click, install this tool and start using in. It is focused on LinkedIn for finding candidates and to automate other recruiting tasks no matter your ability to use technologies for different purposes.

BOOL
Rating: Beginner

Features:
- Quickly build and launch Boolean searches
- Create and save strings
- Keeps you organized
- Easy Chrome extension

This free extension helps create strings and saves them in one convenient place. It's called BOOL (Boolean Search Assistant). It has 4,000 active users and is highly rated by its users. With that in mind, I wanted to do a review of this extension tool.

BOOL is a Chrome extension that streamlines Boolean string construction and x-ray search. The first version was launched in 2016 and has since gone through several iterations. From features such as page analysis and Boolean String Bank integration, the core functionalities have been distilled for greater effectiveness as a search tool.

Whether you are building a target list of companies, titles or skills, BOOL allows you to conveniently and quickly build Boolean strings and launch searches from any window.

How to Use BOOL:
1. Build a Boolean table of AND (blue), OR (green), and NOT (red) rows/columns by clicking the respective buttons.
2. Populate the Boolean table by grouping similar search criteria into the same

columns. Add the required criteria to the blue and green rows (AND and OR) and those not required to the red rows (NOT).
3. Choose the desired search engine, website (for x-ray searches), or filetype (pdf, doc, docx, ppt, or xls).
4. Your Boolean string is built instantly.
5. Quickly run that string search on Google or Bing.
6. Finally, save your search string to the clipboard.

BOOL will continue to evolve as more user-friendly and efficient methods are integrated within the platform. Definitely take the time to write a review in the Chrome store about this tool. The Bool team really appreciates any feedback or thoughts on the tool's functionality.

154

Chapter 9: CRM and ATS Tools

In this chapter we will see different CRM and ATS tools that you can use to track and record your talent sourcing efforts.

Why Do You Need CRM and ATS Tools?
CRM systems work to scale a recruiter's sourcing efforts by attracting passive candidates ahead of demand. In other words, an ATS is a workflow and compliance tool for managing applicants, while a CRM system is a pool of all passive and active candidates, as well as previous applicants already in your system.

So, simply put: these tools are useful to help keep tract of passive and active leads.

Google Sheets
Rating: Beginner
Features:
- Quickly build and launch Boolean searches
- Create and save strings
- Keeps you organized
- Easy Chrome extension

Google Sheets is a spreadsheet program included as part of the free, web-based Google Docs Editors suite offered by Google. The service also includes Google Docs, Google

Slides, Google Drawings, Google Forms, Google Sites, and Google Keep.

Google Sheets makes your data pop with colorful charts and graphs. Built-in formulas, pivot tables and conditional formatting options save time and simplify common spreadsheet tasks. All for free and you can access it in the cloud while creating an account on Google.

You can also choose from a wide variety of budgets, schedules, and other pre-made spreadsheets, all designed to make your work that much better and your life that much easier. Using such a tool will help you stay organized and to collect all the data from the researching in the specific order.

You can open, edit, and save Microsoft Excel files with the Chrome extension or app. It is also free and this is an advantage in comparison with your competitors.

Evernote
Rating: Beginner
Features:
- Save notes with the extension while on individual LinkedIn profiles
- Sync your notes with the web version
- Enhance and save business cards
- Built-in search across documents
- Helpful web clipper for saving information anywhere
- Collaborative tools

There's no doubting Evernote's power when it comes to desktop note-taking, but as a recruiter, being able to sync your notes to the web version will prove that much more useful. In doing so, you'll be able to find anything you save no matter what device you're using.

There's even an integration with LinkedIn that will enhance business cards. Plus, you can automatically start building content-rich notes around every card you scan, including their LinkedIn profile, contact information, photo, and a section for any notes you wish to add yourself.

You also never need Boolean searches to look for information inside of your Evernote account. Simply use the search function that's built-in and you can easily search for candidates, resumes, and notes about your clients. You can even locate PDFs, documents, presentations, and spreadsheets using this search feature.

Search Syntax includes:
- intitle: Searches within the title of the note.
- notebook: Searches for notes stored in the specified notebook.
- any: Searches for notes that match any of the search terms listed.
- tag: Searches for notes tagged with the specified tag.

- -tag: Searches for notes not tagged with the specified tag.
- created: Searches for notes created on or after the date specified.
- updated: Searches for notes updated on or after the date specified.
- resource: Searches for notes that contain specific types of media (audio, images, etc.).
- source: Searches for notes by the application or other source used to create them.
- todo: Searches for notes containing one or more checkboxes.
- encryption: Searches for notes that include text that has been encrypted with Evernote's built-in encryption system.

WhenX

Rating: Beginner
Features:
- Save notes with the extension while on individual LinkedIn profiles.
- Create tasks and get notified via the extension.

With WhenX, keeping track of your LinkedIn candidate notes and Google search results is easy. The tool synchronizes your notes with your Google search, allowing you to share them with your team. The tool also adds timestamps to your previously visited links, making it easy to re-find webpages and giving you a time context of when you searched for certain topics. Features include the ability to easily re-find websites, avoid irrelevant links with recent visit timestamps, and even see timestamps for links visited before installation for a retrospective view.

Chapter 10: Email Automation

The creation of email drip campaigns is crucial in the world of recruiting, as recruiters have adopted this successful concept from the sales industry. Over the years, the sales industry has continuously improved this approach, and recruiters can now fully automate their email sequences when reaching out to and interacting with new candidates.

With various sales and marketing software companies offering excellent tools for creating drip campaigns, it is important to understand the significance of these campaigns and how to set up a sequence using the top email tools available.

Below I will highlight the importance and how to step up a sequence using the top email tools available.

What is an Email Drip Campaign?
The concept of a drip campaign is actually quite simple. In this instance, we're talking about email marketing, where a drip campaign delivers a sequence of messages at certain, pre-specified points in time to help boost engagement and clicks. Recruiters can use these tools to send out scheduled emails and follow-ups to attract and engage a lead.

Drip campaigns are considered more effective than the traditional mail merge email blasts that recruiters have been sending for years now. That's because drip campaigns enable you to get super personal, targeting specific prospects right in their inbox at just the right time.

When it comes to drip campaigns, response and click rates are the number one way to measure success and truly the only metrics that matter the most. An engagement from the recipient truly means that you're sequence campaign has successfully worked.

Constructing an Effective Email Sequence
Constructing an effective sequence happens by trial and error. You will need to slowly experiment on a sequence to see what works and make improvements along the way. Your email should consist of the following components:

Subject Line(s): This is the line your recipient will see before they even open your email. It drives their split-second decisions to read or ignore it.

Connection: The first line in the email is what should grab them to finish reading, so they don't bounce back to their inbox. It should immediately connect to the subject line that got them to open the email. If you sound like an automated robot, odds are your email will get sent to junk.

Question: Once you have established a connection, ask a question. Be clear and upfront. If you have an open position, just say it. Be precise about what you have and create urgency by asking for a response in the next two to three days. Make them seem valued and that you need a response from them as soon as possible.

Email Engagement: Once the lead responds, do you have additional follow-up email templates to address questions or concerns? Also, whichever tool you choose will be a factor in this. Most email sequences will stop or pause the lead responses to the direct email.

When writing your email, remember to focus on common ground to build trust. Including a sincere compliment is also very effective. Ultimately, you need to focus on personalization, which you can still do even if you're marketing at scale.

For instance, if you're reaching out to more than 10 people, you can save time while still maximizing effectiveness by focusing on deeply personalizing the first email each person will receive. From there, you can let automation do more of the work for you, saving time while still making sure that the most important message

– that first email that needs to elicit that first response – is as personal as possible.

Also, remember that simply including an organization or brand name doesn't mean an email has been personalized. You need to do some digging and go beyond that if you truly want the person reading your email to feel that all-important connection that tells them you have actually spent time considering them as an individual.

Gem
Rating: Advanced
Features:
- Sync your notes with the web version
- Enhance and save business cards
- Built-in search across documents
- Helpful web clipper for saving information anywhere
- Collaborative tools

Gem is a customer-oriented, industrial-cutting tool manufacturer located in southeastern Wisconsin. They are specialized in the design and manufacture of carbide, high-speed steel, and diamond tooling for multiple industries. They have the ability to do one-off prototyping as well as large production runs in our facility.

They are able to offer an extensive product and service that is second to none; they have over 3,000 products available to hire and are re-evaluating our fleet to ensure they keep up to date with the latest technological advances and latest regulations. With Gem, it is possible to hire anything from wallpaper strippers through to diggers, access equipment, and much more.

Interstellar

Rating: Advanced
Features:
- Sync your notes with the web version
- Enhance and save business cards
- Built-in search across documents
- Helpful web clipper for saving information anywhere
- Collaborative tools

Reaching out to candidates shouldn't require a dozen processes and tools. Interstellar is a great tool for you for these purposes. Interstellar is a simple solution for all your email needs. There are a lot of features, such as:

1. Source - Source your own candidates using our Chrome extension or upload a list of contacts to add to an email sequence.

2. Outreach - Add candidates into an email sequence to automate a series of personalized emails that are sent directly to a contact's inbox.

3. Connect - Synchronize all your candidates and communication to your current services. Connect a dozen native integrations.

This Chrome extension is easy to use, and you can install it with one click on the Chrome extensions field.

Resource.io

Rating: Beginner

Features:
- Sync your notes with the web version
- Enhance and save business cards
- Built-in search across documents
- Helpful web clipper for saving information anywhere
- Collaborative tools

Supercharge your sourcing and book more interviews with the all-in-one Outreach and CRM platform for recruiting teams. Say goodbye to messaging channels that don't work. Say hello to one-click outreach and email automation for any profile on the web.

Stand out with the perfect message at the perfect time and make a first impression that's impossible to ignore. Build relationships with powerful follow-ups, and nurture campaigns to improve conversion rates.

Here's all the features:

1. Contact data - Save time with automated, best-in-class contact data.

2. Open tracking - Know who opened your email and when for perfectly timed follow-ups.

3. Templates - Avoid copy and pasting with rich email templates for every occasion.

4. Smart follow-ups - Increase responses and stay top of mind with intelligent follow-ups.

5. Contact upload - Upload a list of contacts from any source to start building relationships.

6. Team collaboration - Get your whole company involved in sourcing while maintaining full control.

7. ATS integration - Nurture applicants and log outreach automatically with two-way ATS Sync.

8. Rich insights - Understand your team's performance with powerful insights.

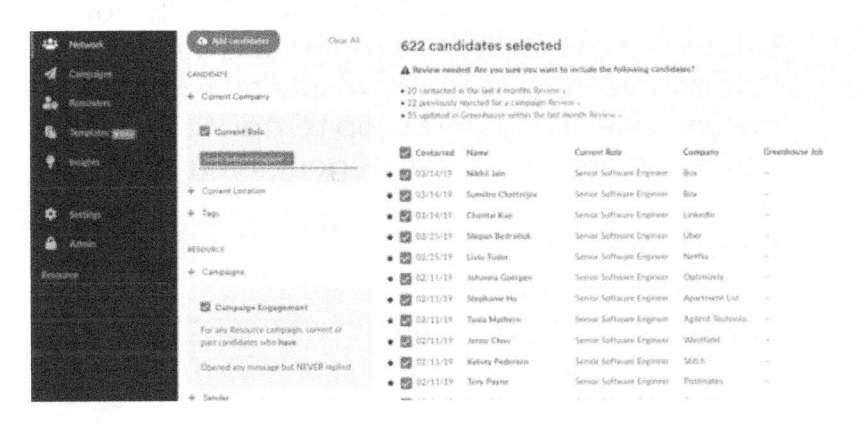

Lemlist
Rating: Advanced
Features:
- Sync your notes with the web version
- Enhance and save business cards
- Built-in search across documents

- Helpful web clipper for saving information anywhere

Send cold emails that get replies. A tool to power sales teams, agencies, and B2B businesses personalize and automate cold emails.

Connect your email account in seconds. It doesn't matter what email provider you use; we support all of them. Take a few seconds to connect and Lemlist syncs smoothly with your email account.

Add a much-needed personal touch without sacrificing the ability to send emails at scale. Communicate with your prospects on a one-on-one level. Drag-and-drop template collection organized in categories you need:

- Sales
- Follow-ups
- Backlink generation
- Talent Sourcing

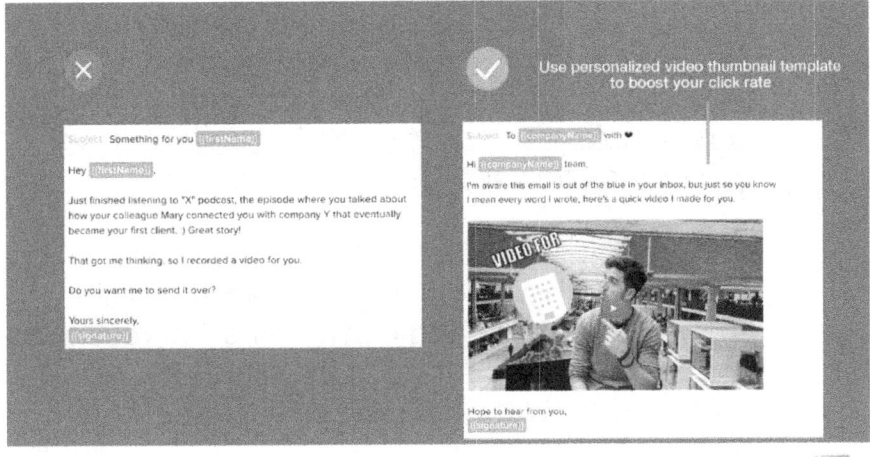

Trinsly
Rating: Beginner
Features:
- Sync your notes with the web version
- Enhance and save business cards
- Built-in search across documents
- Helpful web clipper for saving information anywhere
- Collaborative tools

Supercharge your sourcing and business development to get more placements. Send personalized reach outs that automatically follows up directly from LinkedIn, ATS, or any website.

Following up three times in two weeks doubles your response rate. Trinsly takes care of follow-ups that stop when prospects reply.

No more Excel spreadsheets, copying and pasting messages, setting reminders, or switching to your ATS. Understand and personalize reach outs directly from wherever you found the candidate.

This is a paid tool, for $59, you can get a Solo package with a 10-day free trial and unlimited email researching and campaigns. There is an option to integrate it into Gmail and Microsoft Office 365 so you will level up in front of the competitors.

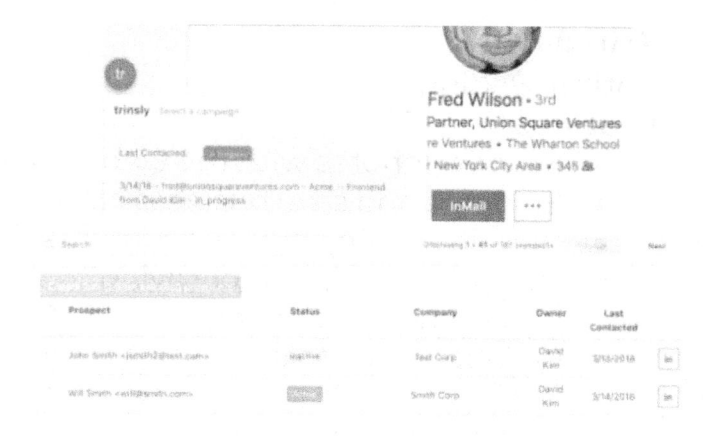

Mail Merge (Old School)
Rating: Beginner
Features:
- Sync your notes with the web version
- Enhance and save business cards
- Built-in search across documents
- Helpful web clipper for saving information anywhere

Mail merge lets you create a batch of documents that are personalized for each recipient. For example, a form letter might be personalized to address each recipient by name. A data source, like a list, spreadsheet, or database, is associated with the document.

Mail merge lets you personalize emails with a single data file and a single email template. The data is picked from the file and is inserted automatically at specific places in the template.

If you are not sure how to use mail merge, your best bet is Gmail. You can use mail merge with Gmail easily and make your emails personalized. You can use a single email template and customize it to a great extent with this amazing feature. Mail merge with Gmail is free to use and provides you with decent personalization features.

Using and installing this tool is a simple process. Download the Mail Merge with attachments Chrome extension. It is a free extension that lets you use mail merge right from your Gmail dashboard.

After that, start using it with one click and you will see the results as soon as possible.

Mailchimp
Rating: Beginner
Features:
- Free for up to 2,000 subscribers

- Setup is simple and user-friendly
- You can group your lists
- Feed merge tags to customize content

Once you have an account created, the first step will be creating different group lists. Create different group lists based on job-opening categories for example:

- Marketing Opportunities List
- Finance Opportunities List
- SAP Opportunities

I would encourage you to have that lead directly subscribe to your newsletter. Here's an example message you could use on LinkedIn:

> Jonathan, it was a real pleasure speaking with you about your future plans. I will be sending a bi-monthly newsletter about our career opportunities at our company.
>
> Please keep me updated on your future goals and let me know if any of these openings would be of interest to you.
>
> (Click here to opt in for our "Marketing" careers newsletter)

I recommend creating a unique template for each group list job category. You could highlight employer branding content, for example: projects that department is working on, PR related news, or employer branding videos. Make sure your email campaigns are relevant to the demographic you are targeting.

Once you've created those different group lists and have around 15-20 subscribers, you can then schedule email campaign blast to go out on a future date. You can read how to schedule an email campaign here. When you've included in the RSS channel tags, this email campaign could become completely automated.

By using Mailchimp, you basically automate your future talent pipeline! You can keep passive talent warm for several months with little effort. This will help increase your future applications. You can even get more creative by asking for referrals and encouraging your subscribers to share the job openings with their networks on social media.

Saleshandy
Rating: Intermediate
Features:
- Track clicks and views on emails
- Mass mail merge features
- Create up to six email sequences
- Find Email address on LinkedIn profiles

Deep personalization, more replies

Standardize your outreach strategy with the power of personalization. Saleshandy helps to personalize your email and subject lines with merge tags to get more replies with improved results.

Effortless automation on follow-ups
Autopilot your cold email outreach with the help of automated follow-ups. Schedule multi-stage sequences in advance to receive high open rates and generate more conversations to improve your conversion.

One-click integration with your Email Service Provider
Set up cold emailing without interrupting your workflow. Easily integrate Saleshandy with your email service provider to save time on switching between apps and improve your productivity.

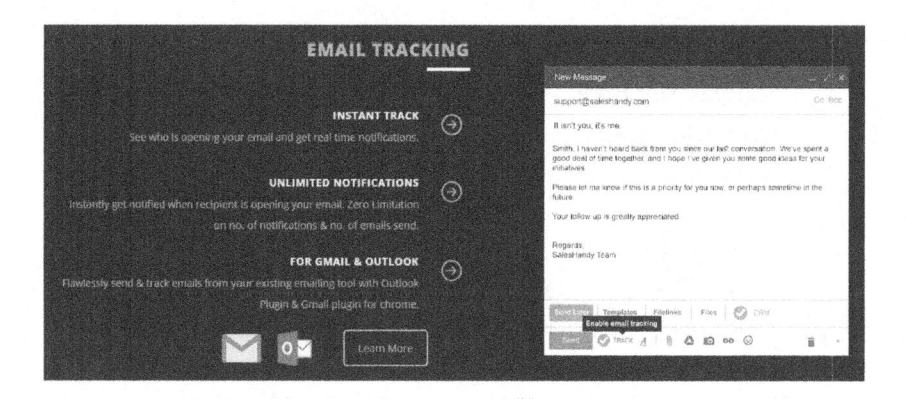

Chapter 11: Email Tracking Tools

Are you searching for the best option to track your emails? If yes, then these tools are for you. Recruiting involves a lot of going through back and forth over email with applicants. So, knowing that the recipient is viewing and responding to your emails is important.

Why Do You Need Email Tracking Tools?
The same way email marketers track open rates you can do the same for recruiting. Our industry is ever-changing and the lines between marketing and recruiting continue to blend together. By tracking, you can see if applicants are viewing your emails. Communicating can be the biggest time sucker so having a tool that tracks views/response can come in handy.

The email tracking tools place an invisible image inside your emails and once the recipient clicks/opens the email, you will be notified. The users will not know that they are being tracked. These tools will help you with it.

Clearbit
Rating: Beginner
Features:
- Data engine interaction
- Search your future customers

Clearbit is the marketing data engine for all of your customer interactions. Deeply understand your customers, identify future prospects, and personalize every single marketing and sales interaction.

Rely on fresh, accurate data with our proprietary real-time lookups. Then act on new information immediately, with sales alerting and job change notifications.

Get company attributes like employee count, technologies used, and industry classification and get employee details like role, seniority, and even job change notifications, right at your fingertips.

With our dataset and machine learning algorithms, you'll have all of the information you need to convert leads and grow your business.

Get the right data directly into the tools you already use. They built Clearbit from the ground up to integrate right into your existing stack, providing uniform, seamless data across your sales, marketing, and analytics teams.

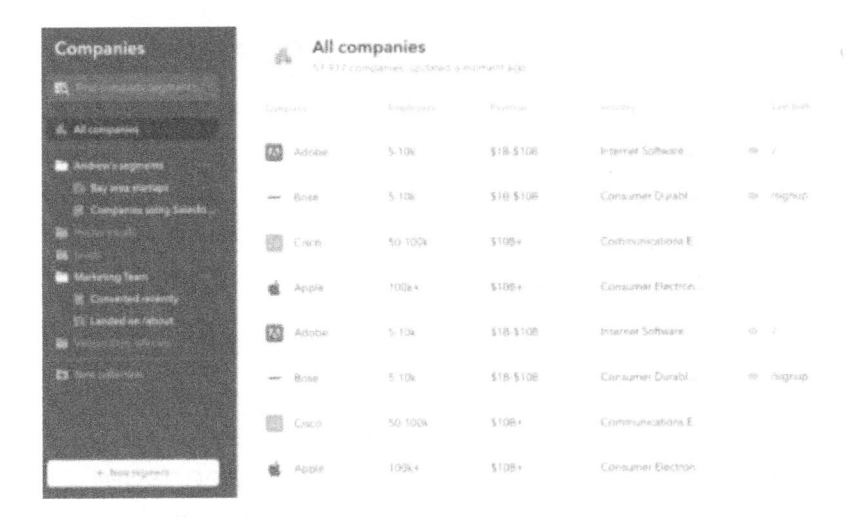

FullContact

Rating: Beginner
Features:
- Different media integration
- Graphs and charts for clients' identities
- B2B connections with people and brands

Empower connections between people and brands. This tool is a person-first identity resolution platform that provides the crucial intelligence needed to drive data onboarding, media amplification, omnichannel measurement, and customer recognition.

Gain unparalleled recognition and insights by mapping fragmented identities into a persistent PersonID with our person-first identity graph. There are 275 million whole-person profiles. Over 50 billion individual omnichannel identifiers that is amazing information that will give you advantage in front of your competitors.

There are also 70,000+ ethically-sourced personal and professional attributes on every USA-based consumer. It will for sure help you in your business purposes and bring you a huge benefit.

Increase your conversions and improve the lifetime value of your relationships by recognizing your customers as they engage with your brand. There are 40 millisecond response time and 30+ million updates per day.

Your data is your data – it's never commingled or added to our graph, and you have total control over who has access to it, as well as the confidence levels of identity matching. The private identity cloud secures your data and reduces risk, all in a privacy-compliant manner.

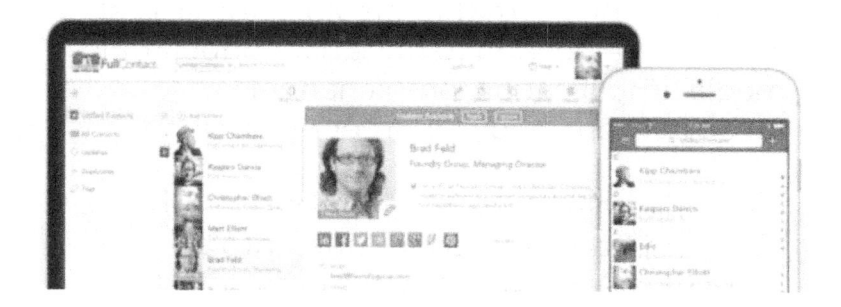

Streak for Gmail
Rating: Beginner
Features:
- Integration with different email platforms
- Awarded best Chrome tool by Google
- Use this as a CRM to track candidates
- Track email open and click rates

Receive a notification when your proposal is viewed, and you'll know exactly when to follow up. Know if your email is read and not responded to or never reaches the recipient. Streak offers many other features besides tracking, so it's worth reviewing further.

Manage sales and customer relationships directly inside Gmail. Streak is Google's 2018 Technology G Suite Partner of the Year! You can manage your CRM or any workflow directly within Gmail.

Stop switching back and forth between your inbox and other tools. Set up for you and your team a perfect process for numerous use-cases, including Sales, Partnerships, Support, Hiring, and more.

They are trusted and loved by teams across every industry:
- 750,000 users, 4.5 stars on Google Chrome store
- Used by teams at Uber, Keller Williams, WeWork, TechStars, Atlassian, Lyft, The

Economist, Y-Combinator, and many more

Built into the tools you already use. Work where you already are inside your inbox. Built directly inside of Gmail for desktop and mobile, with G Suite integrations (Sheets, Chat, Drive and more) to help you access and gather your data quickly.

This tool will enable you to easily collaborate and share emails, notes, call logs with your team so you can pick up where they left off. Access pipeline data alongside your emails and from your pocket so you always have the context you need.

Streak is like a pipeline on autopilot. Automatically capture data from the contacts and emails you send and receive in your pipelines. Get notified as leads progress through your pipeline and never forget to follow up with tasks and reminders.

There is a chance for you to supercharge your inbox with email power tools. Manage your conversations at scale and eliminate repetitive emails using Snippets and Mail Merge. Schedule crucial emails for the appropriate time using Send Later, and know exactly when to follow up with Email Tracking. Keep conversations on point by separating email threads where conversations flow using Thread Splitter.

This tool is native for Android and iOS apps and you can use it worldwide. Comprehensive integrations with G Suite, Zapier and APIs to connect to everything you need to. Also, Streak is built in the same cloud as Gmail and G Suite which is an awesome feature and use for many purposes.

Bananatag for Gmail and Outlook
Rating: Beginner
Features:
- Automatic tracking
- Track views and number of clicks

They will send you a notification to your inbox when a contact opens your email or clicks a link. Emails tracked with Bananatag look no different to recipients and arrive from your address.

See what happens to your personal emails after you press send. Email Tracking shows you when your emails are opened and when recipients click links in the body of your email. Seamlessly track any email you send. Emails tracked with Bananatag look no different to recipients and arrive from your address.

Track any email with a single click, right from inside the compose window. All links are automatically tracked too. Once tracked, emails are sent through your own server so they arrive from your email address, and your data is always secure. Tracked email metrics provide stats on overall interaction with your emails and help you make your emails better.

There are two subscription plans you can choose to start using this tool. The first one is called pro and it costs $12.50 per month where you will get:

- Track up to 100 Emails Daily
- Detailed Notifications
- Full Email Metrics
- Email Scheduling
- Email Templates
- Attachment Tracking
- Custom Reports

The second is called Teams and it costs $25 per month with the features:

- Track up to 200 Emails Daily

- Detailed Notifications
- Full Email Metrics
- Email Scheduling
- Email Templates
- Team Email Templates
- Attachment Tracking

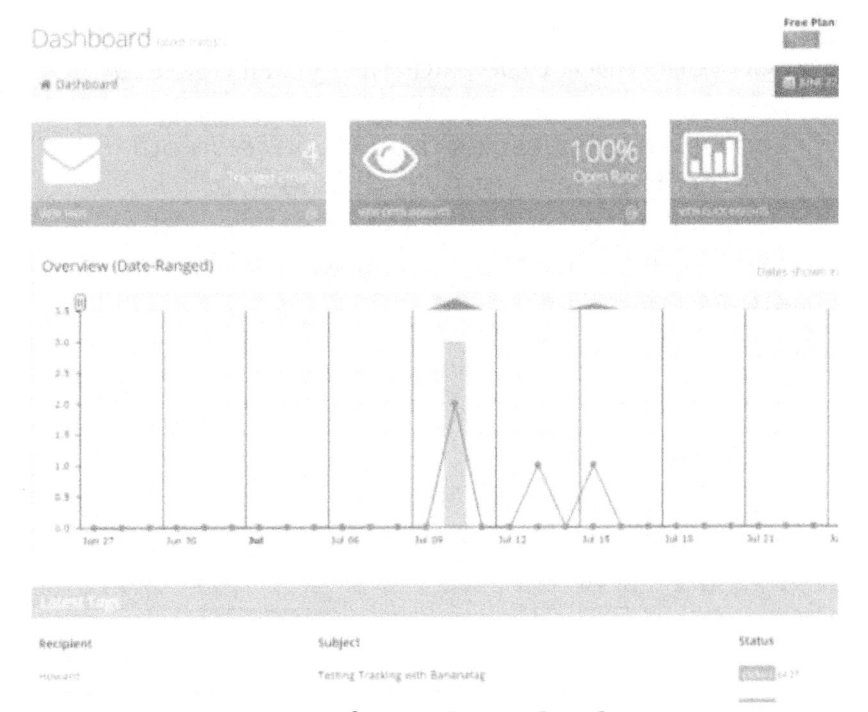

Yesware for Gmail and Outlook
Rating: Beginner
Features:
- Multiple platforms integration
- Simple to install
- Easily track all your open and clicks within the tool

Know who opens your emails and clicks on your links. It's simple and user-friendly. Installing Yesware is extremely simple and takes no more than about a minute. You can install Yesware directly from our website.

They offer a trial to all new users that can be accessed here. Once you visit that link, click on your inbox type and then you'll need to sign into your email and grant Yesware access. It's as easy as that! If you're on our Enterprise plan, you will also need to authenticate to Salesforce (essentially sign in and grant access), and you will be prompted to do so.

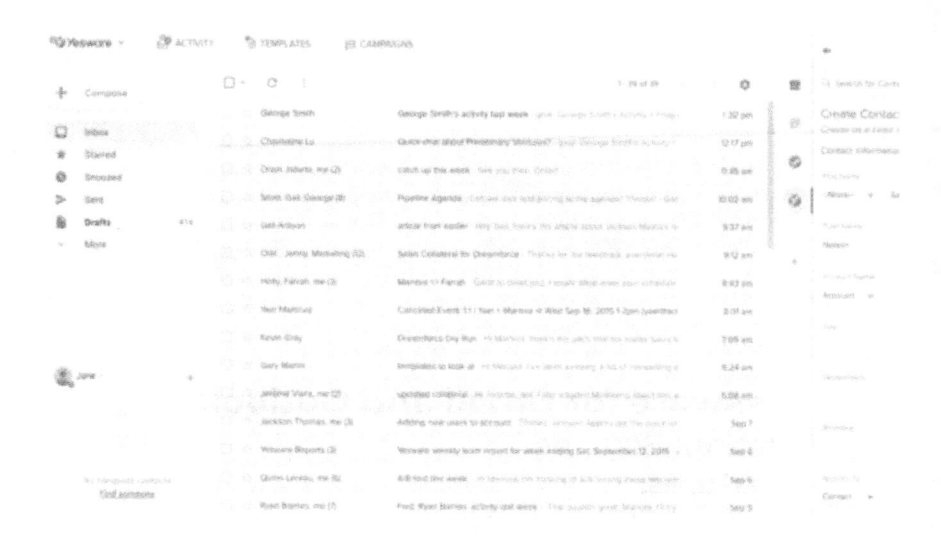

Mailtrack for Gmail and Outlook
Rating: Beginner
Features:
- Tracking any email address

- Easy installation and simple to use

You can see if your emails have been opened in your mailbox. This is another one that's simple and easy to use.

Mailtrack works seamlessly with Gmail, but you can use another email client for email tracking in Outlook or Yahoo, for example.

Mailtrack is only available to download as a Gmail email tracker extension through Chrome or as an add-on for the Gmail Android and iOS app.

However, there is another way that you can use Mailtrack for email tracking in Outlook and other email clients, by using the Gmailify option included in Gmail.

You can use Mailtrack as an email tracker for other addresses, as long as they are rerouted through Gmail. Let's cover exactly how to do that.

1. Get a Gmail account (if you don't already have one): To use this tool, you need to have a Gmail account. You can set one up for free. Don't worry; you can still use your Outlook or Yahoo email address. In other words, no one will ever know you are using a Gmail address.

2. Navigate to account settings: Go to Gmail and click the gear icon, then click "See all settings." Then, click on "Accounts and Import."

3. Add your other email account: Scroll to "Check mail from other accounts" and click "Add a mail account." Next, enter the address for your other account. Select "Link accounts with Mailtrack," click next, and then log in with your account credentials. When complete, you'll see the successful message.

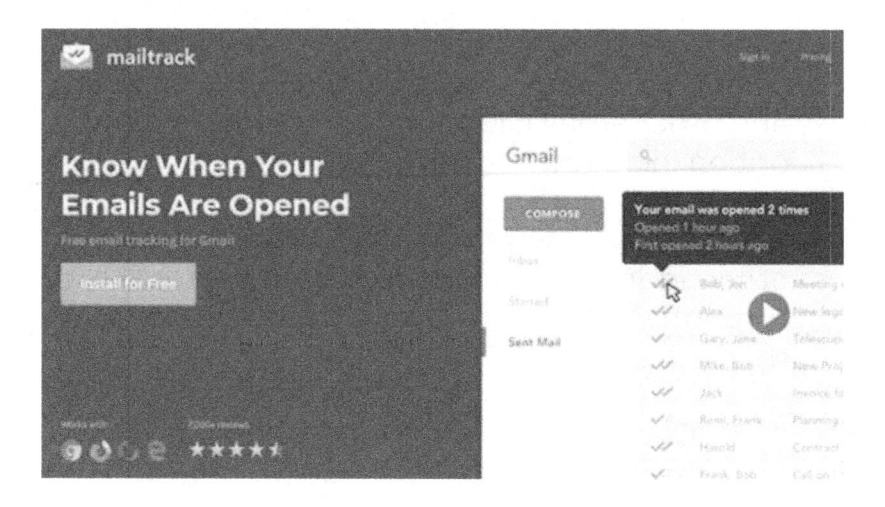

ContactMonkey for Gmail and Outlook

Rating: Beginner

Features:
- Tracking other email using your inbox
- Allows you to send pre-saved email templates
- Boost your engagement

See who's opening your email right from your inbox. Track your emails from the comfort of your Gmail inbox.

ContactMonkey is built into your Gmail inbox so you can start tracking in seconds. No need to learn any new programs. Just install and start tracking emails right away.

Know exactly when your emails have been opened, clicked, from where and on which device. It is a perfect tool for internal communicators who want to boost employee engagement from Gmail.

Gmail Mail Merge is streamlined for simplicity, so you can send in seconds and track every last email. Gmail delay send lets you specify the timing down to the minute.

Use the simple stats dashboard to see your top email subject lines, links, cities, and more. Open the graph analytics to get an overview of what's working – and what isn't – at a glance.

Re: What'd you think of our e-book?

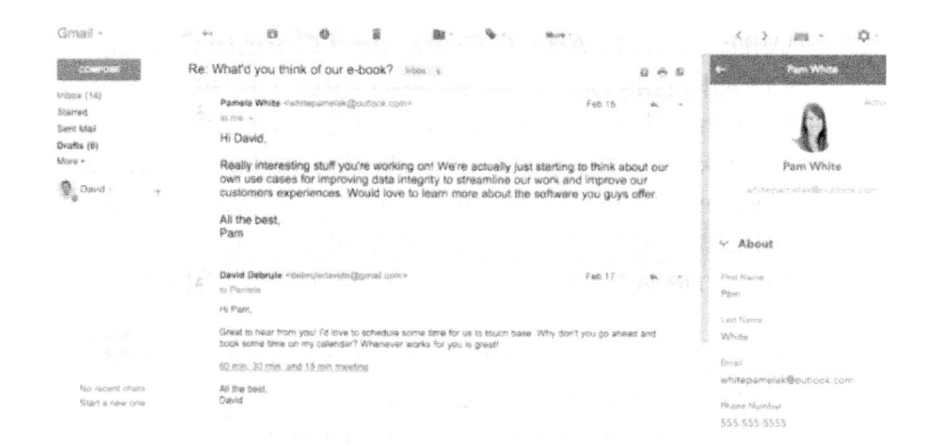

Pamela White <whitepamelak@outlook.com>
to me
Feb 15

Hi David,

Really interesting stuff you're working on! We're actually just starting to think about our own use cases for improving data integrity to streamline our work and improve our customers experiences. Would love to learn more about the software you guys offer.

All the best,
Pam

David Debrule <debruledavide@gmail.com>
to Pamela
Feb 17

Hi Pam,

Great to hear from you! I'd love to schedule some time for us to touch base. Why don't you go ahead and book some time on my calendar? Whenever works for you is great!

60 min, 30 min, and 15 min meetings

All the best,
David

Pam White

About

First Name
Pam

Last Name
White

Email
whitepamelak@outlook.com

Phone Number
555-555-5555

Chapter 12: People Search Engines

In this chapter, we will talk about more tools regarding People Search Engines and how these tools will help you build a larger network and find more potential candidates on the web.

Why Use a People Search Engines?

Having a difficult time finding a candidate's contact information? Well, people search engines were designed to give you this type of confidential information.

A people search engine is a type of search engine that specializes in finding information about individuals. It is designed to help users locate and gather information about specific people, such as their name, address, phone number, occupation, education, and social media profiles. People search engines typically use publicly available information from sources such as social media, online directories, and government records to compile comprehensive profiles on individuals. They can be useful for a variety of purposes, including background checks, genealogy research, locating lost friends or family members, and more.

These search engines fall into two categories:

Primary Site Characteristics:

• Get their information more-or-less directly from public record sources.
• Collect data through some human activities, such as going to a local courthouse.
• Generally, more accurate than secondary sites.
• Examples include: Intelius, LexisNexis, and PeopleFinders.

Secondary Site Characteristics:
• Aggregate their information from primary sites, social networks, and other online sources.
• Collect data automatically, through electronic means
• Known for being fairly accurate.
• Examples include: Spokeo, Pipl, and Radaris.

They usually have your name, other names you've gone by, where you currently live, where you used to live, your phone number, your family members, your birth date and age, your criminal record, the real estate you own, and more.

Where do People Search Engines get this information from?

• Real estate transactions (including appraisals)
• Trademark filings
• Marriage licenses and divorce decrees
• Any unsealed lawsuits or legal actions
• Birth certificates
• Death certificates
• Census statistics
• Voter registrations

- Drivers licenses
- Utility companies
- Government spending reports
- Political campaign contributions
- Sex offender registrations
- Legislation minutes
- Business and entity filings
- Professional and business licenses

Pipl Pro
Rating: Advanced
Features:
- Find contact and personal info for your candidates
- Search LinkedIn profiles using LinkedIn URLs

I recently came across this tool during a discussion on the Recruiting Leaders group on Facebook. Someone was trying to get more information on Pipl search engine's Pro version. I honestly didn't realize Pipl offered a paid version. I've been using the free version for a couple years now. As of 2017, Pipl quietly launched a full PRO version of their services.

Pipl is actually the largest People Search Engine in the world, providing users with the ability to search over 3 billion people worldwide. Basically, they index information from millions of sources and provide users with the ability to connect online identities with real people.

They help banks, insurance, and e-commerce companies with identity verification to reduce fraud. Only within the past few years have recruiters and sourcers been using Pipl search to find candidate contact information. So, with the permission of Pipl, I was granted full access to test out all the features.

Here's what you can search on Pipl Pro:
- **Name:** (First then last name).
- **Email Address:** use this to cross reference for additional information.
- **Using Usernames:** This is a unique identifier for finding someone's info based off username ID's. Such as (username@linkedin, Username@facebook, Username@twitter). It can track different IP's and find that individuals contact information. Just copy the URL from LinkedIn or Facebook and paste in the Pipl Pro search bar and the Pipl Pro will give you an immediate response. **For example:** my Facebook ID is Facebook.com/JonathanEdwardKidder – you can find my contact information when you copy and paste my ID into the search bar.
- **Phone Number:** (area code and phone number, country code not necessary, just remember the more information the better the result).
- **There is an advanced search:** you can find the advanced search in two places.

194

When you type in a name and search, look to the left of the screen and look for more options. Click more options, you will also notice you can search by regions and ages on the left. Once you click advanced searches, see how the screen allows for more detailed information.

My final thoughts on Pipl Pro
I've been able to demo Pipl Pro for about a week now. I am truly amazed by what this tool can do. I would say it was at least 80 percent accurate for finding cell numbers and email addresses. If you have a budget, the first level accounts cost $99-149 for 200 searches a month and it's definitely worth the value.

Jonathan E Kidder
28 years old

Male, Speaks English
Born January 31, 1989
From **White Bear Lake**, **Minnesota** and 5 more places

CAREER
Sr. Talent Acquisition Sourcer + Employer Branding Specialist at Vista Outdoor Inc.
Employer Branding + Talent Acquisition Sourcer at Vista Outdoor Inc.
Senior Talent Acquisition Sourcer at Vista Outdoor Inc. (since 2016)
Senior Talent Acquisition Sourcer at G & K Services (2016-2016)
Talent Acquisition Sourcer at G & K Services (2016-2016)
14 more »

EDUCATION
Marketing, Business from Bethel University (2007-2011)

ZoomInfo
Rating: Advanced
Features:

- Great for contacting client and company intel
- Gives ORG information
- Accuracy levels 80-90 percent

Source Qualified Candidates

As a recruiter, you need to know who to reach and how to reach them. ZoomInfo Recruiter offers talent acquisition professionals 360-degree sourcing intelligence, including:

- **Contact information:** Mobile phone numbers and personal email addresses
- **Candidate details:** Job functions, titles, and years of experience
- **Roles and responsibilities:** Department org charts, technology skills, and professional certifications

Ben Arnold
Marketing Manager, ACME Tech.

Detailed candidate history

CONTACT

Mobile
307-948-1832

Business
307-948-1832

Personal
ben.arn@gmail.com

Business
barnold@acme.co

EMPLOYMENT HISTORY

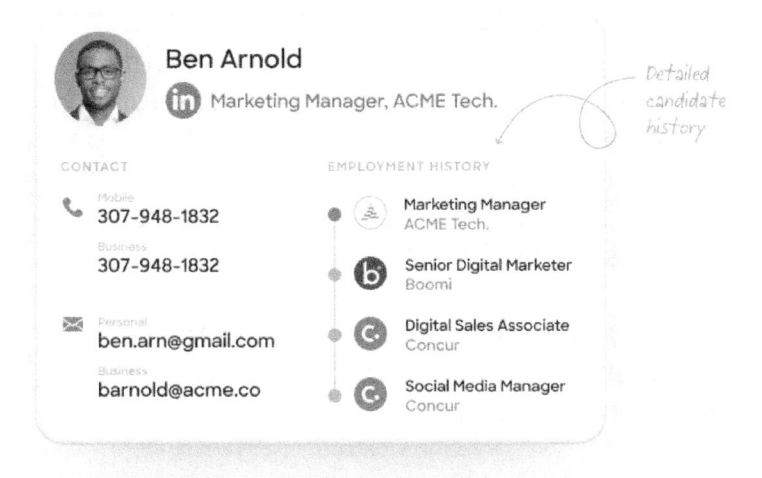

Marketing Manager
ACME Tech.

Senior Digital Marketer
Boomi

Digital Sales Associate
Concur

Social Media Manager
Concur

Intelius
Rating: Beginner
Features:
- Find information on who contacted you
- Often updates – has many verified sources

Intelius provides information services, including people and property search, background checks and reverse phone lookup.

At Intelius, they aim to keep you informed. Since being founded in 2003, they have continued to offer the most reliable place to search for people, telephone numbers, addresses, background checks, criminal records, and more.

Whether you want to reunite with your college roommate or learn more about the person your daughter is dating, Intelius is your go-to resource for finding people. They are continuously updating the people search engine to provide you with an accurate and robust set of information.

1. Safety - Quickly get the information you need, and be empowered to make the right decisions to stay safe.

2. Anonymity - All searches are private and completely confidential. No one will know you searched for them.

3. Knowledge - With over 20 billion available public records, Intelius provides access to the best information available online.

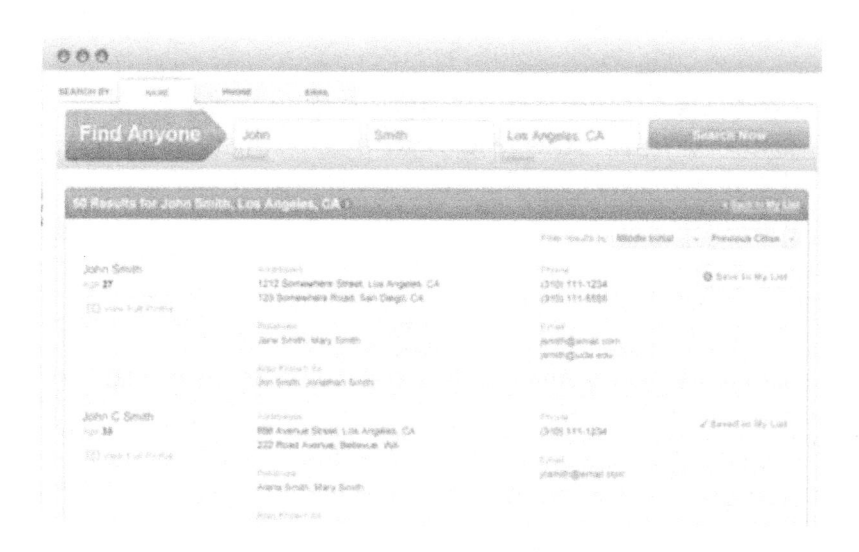

LinkedIn

Rating: Advanced

Features:
- Large pool of talent professional network
- Reach a large talent pool quickly

The platform is mainly used for professional networking and allows job seekers to post their CVs and employers to post jobs.

LinkedIn allows members (both workers and employers) to create profiles and connect to each other in an online social network which may represent real-world professional relationships. Members can invite anyone (whether an existing member or not) to become a connection.

LinkedIn applications often refers to external third-party applications that interact with LinkedIn's developer API. However, in some cases, it could refer to sanctioned applications featured on a user's profile page.

LinkedIn is free to use, you just need to sign up for a new profile on the official website. Also, there are paid features you can activate for better and advanced researching and analytical purposes.

LexisNexis Public Records

Rating: Beginner

Features:
- Search internationally
- Large searchable database

Uncover hidden connections between people, companies, and assets that could impact your business. Locate elusive people, businesses, and assets wherever they may hide. Follow the footprints – addresses, employers, social media accounts and even associates – with flags, filters and alerts that keep the trail hot.

Nothing escapes your notice. LexID advanced linking technology surfaces relationships between people, businesses and locations even when they don't appear together in a public records document.

Discover fast, flexible ways to perform due diligence, litigation discovery, or competitive research. Then roll up your findings into an extensive yet easy-to-read SmartLinx® report for your paper trail. Done and done.

Uncover more with LexisNexis Public Records. Click a state to see the critical information advantages LexisNexis holds over the competition in your state.

Motor vehicle records in Maryland. Judgments and liens in Texas. Criminal court files in California. No matter where your research takes you, LexisNexis gives you the edge with exclusive content and bigger, deeper archives in a host of categories.

To start using it, just sign up for a free account and enjoy in your researching activities.

PeopleSmart
Rating: Beginner
Features:
- Find phone numbers
- Get real-time insights

Reach the right people with the right message, and empower your business growth. Whether you're looking to target new sales, refresh your contact lists, or enhance your company data – they've got you covered.

Their proprietary confidence scoring algorithm will suggest the best available contact information for your search and clearly sort it by confidence level so that you can connect easier and faster than ever before.

Leverage more than just basic contact information. Learn more about your customers and their needs with extensive reports on people, phone numbers, email addresses and even social media profiles.

1. Accurate, reliable phone numbers to help you easily connect with your next sale.
2. Search their LinkedIn profile and you might discover even more about them.

3. No more wading through out-of-date company directories.
4. Understand their role, company, and professional history.
5. Mitigate your risk by verifying customers and matching transaction data.

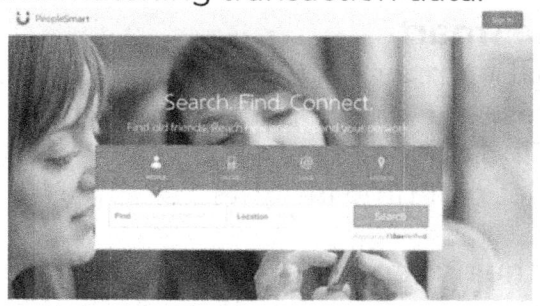

Yasni
Rating: Beginner
Features:
- Social media integration
- Matching candidates by specific keywords
- Reputation Management features

Yasni is a German people search engine operated by yasni GmbH. It aggregates search results from external sources and is, therefore a Meta search engine.

Yasni was founded in 2007 by Steffen Rühl. In 2008, the Swiss Mountain Business Angels came on board as an investor group, whereupon Yasni expanded and went online with an international version in 19 regions and 14 languages.

Besides the simple search, there is also the possibility of regularly receiving newly found search results by email or to actively place a missing person ad. With the so-called PeopleSearch, Yasni developed a tool in 2009 to find people that match with certain keywords.

Yasni enables its users to register a user account and add the already found search results to it. With extended features such as adding links, texts, images or the creation of a business card, Yasni allows people to differentiate themselves from namesakes and pursue active reputation management.

With all that, Yasni also allows its users the popular communication and interlinking possibilities of a social network.

FreshAddress
Rating: Beginner
Features:
- Clean and verify your email list
- Build your email list

Make regular email hygiene the foundation of your email marketing program. Correct hygiene errors, avoid blacklists and improve deliverability by removing bouncing email addresses, disposable domains, and toxic but deliverable spamtraps, honeypots, and frequent spam complainers with our SafeToSend email validation service.

FreshAddress has the tools you need to reconnect with customers lost to bouncing or inactive email addresses, keep your clean email lists problem-free, and protect your SafeToSend investment. Take the next step in email retention and hygiene by keeping your lists up to date with the tools patented Email Change of Address (ECOA) and List Guard services.

FreshAddress delivers customer acquisition solutions that help you reach more customers in their inbox or mailbox. The tools data appending services add opted-in email addresses to your existing postal database as well as postal information to your existing email address database.

Also, there are many free tools which you can use here so it's worth checking them up. If you want to start using, just sign up for a free account and enjoy.

EmailSherlock
Rating: Beginner
Features:
- Email researching
- Verify emails quickly

You can do a free email search on EmailSherlock.com. A reverse email search conducted at EmailSherlock.com can help determine the identity of the owner of an unknown address that shows up in your inbox. You can also use this free email search service to learn more about an address you found in your address book or perhaps in connection with an online ad you're considering responding to.

Now with this handy Chrome tool, you can right-click any email address and directly search it on EmailSherlock.com or select any text and EmailSherlock will find the email address in the context and show you the direct search box for it.

EmailSherlock allows you to search for information regarding the owner of a real email address. More than one billion Facebook users, in addition to millions using other social networks such as Flickr, Foursquare, and Vimeo. Must use a real email address to become registered users on these sites. This means that EmailSherlock can search these databases and check to find any online profile connected to the email address you're searching.

EmailSherlock provides a free email search for you to use at will, checking as many or few email addresses you please. No hidden fees means that you can easily and quickly determine who is sending you questionable emails. Conducting a reverse email address search can help you avoid getting scammed by bogus email addresses asking for money or personal information since many of these types of emails are illegitimate and lead to nowhere.

Spokeo
Rating: Beginner
Features:
- Search for full contact information
- Find location information on leads
- Cross reference contact details with a lead

Search by name, phone, address, or email to confidentially look up information about people you know such as yourself, friends, family, acquaintances, and old classmates.

Look up results from a wide range of industry-leading data sources and, where available, combine all the data into an easy-to-understand report in seconds:

- 130 Million Property Records
- 6 Billion Consumer Records
- Billions of Historical Records
- 600 Million Court Records
- 89 Million Business Records
- 120+ Social Networks

People increasingly mistrust companies, technologies, and each other. They want to leverage data to make the world around us more transparent – making trust a little easier.

Spokeo is a people intelligence service that helps you search, connect, and know who you are dealing with. You can use it to find old friends, identify unknown callers, or research your date. Professionals use it to find new customers or to prevent fraud. Knowledge is a quick search away.

They organize over 12 billion records from thousands of data sources into easy-to-understand reports that include available contact information, location history, photos, social media accounts, family members, court records, work information, and much more. They help you know more, assisting your internal compass to point true north.

Also, there are many free tools which you can use, so it's worth checking them out. If you want to start, just sign up for a free account and enjoy.

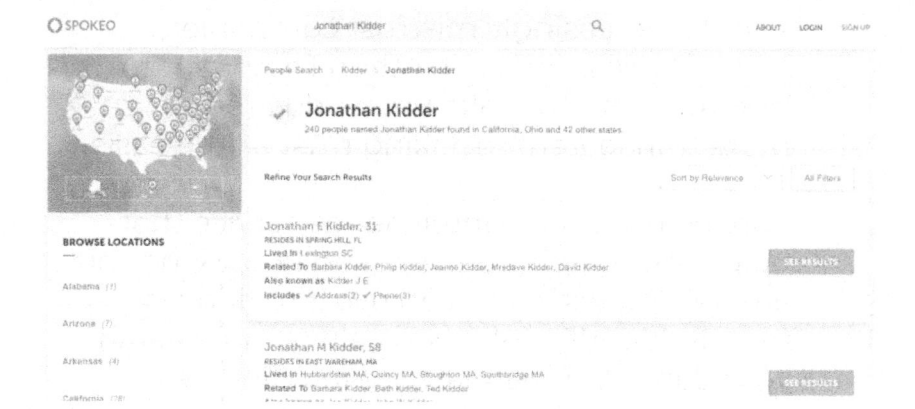

SPOKEO

Jonathan Kidder

ABOUT   LOGIN   SIGN UP

People Search › Kidder › Jonathan Kidder

Jonathan Kidder
240 people named Jonathan Kidder found in California, Ohio and 42 other states.

Refine Your Search Results   Sort by Relevance   All Filters

BROWSE LOCATIONS

Alabama (1)

Arizona (7)

Arkansas (4)

California (28)

Jonathan E Kidder, 31
RESIDES IN SPRING HILL, FL
Lived In Lexington SC
Related To Barbara Kidder, Philip Kidder, Jeanne Kidder, Mredave Kidder, David Kidder
Also known as Kidder J E
Includes ✓ Address(2) ✓ Phone(3)

SEE RESULTS

Jonathan M Kidder, 58
RESIDES IN EAST WAREHAM, MA
Lived In Hubbardston MA, Quincy MA, Stoughton MA, Southbridge MA
Related To Barbara Kidder, Beth Kidder, Ted Kidder

SEE RESULTS

Chapter 13: Chapter: Data/Tracking Tools

Recruiting is a lot like fishing. When reaching out to leads, it's a combination of luck and timing. Sometimes you catch great leads who are open to looking at new opportunities. The more you can plan ahead and prepare yourself, the better response you will have back.

Why Do You Need Data/Tracking Tools?
There's a lot of different tools that you can track users over social media. You can see when they update their LinkedIn profile summaries, resumes, or just websites in general.

Blogtrottr
Rating: Beginner
Features:
- Tracking information
- Easy and free to use

As the name suggests, Blogtrottr delivers fresh and nutritious news to your inbox. What makes them different? So, they send you the things you need, at your convenience. Rather than having to constantly scour blogs and websites, (and forget half the ones you follow) this tool will automatically mail you updates from your own personal selection, on schedules that you choose.

Get RSS and Atom feeds from your favorite websites and blogs sent to your email account in real-time, for free. Use this to track clients or candidates with blogs. This tool supports PubSubHubbub for super quick notifications where you can get your emails within seconds, not hours.

You can have your updates singly and as they happen or wrapped up in a variety of digests. Let your email client do the hard work – customizable email subjects allow easy manipulation by your email client.

Only get the content you want. Blogtrottr filters enable you to include or exclude updates based on the item contents. Easily share content with your friends via our selection of social media buttons.

HTML emails too much for your device? No problem, they can serve you up some plain text too. Have your updates sent as a PDF or as plain text or HTML (with embedded images) attachments for easy offline or e-book reading.

This is a paid tool and there is an option to start a free trial.

For $15.99 per year, you will get all kinds of marketing material and features, such as keyword filters and similar, that will help you for audience engaging.

For $39.99 per year, you will get the lite package, where it comes with 250 subscriptions and dozens of other advanced features.

Lastly, for $69.99 per year, you will get unlimited subscriptions and credits with unlimited advanced marketing features and tools.

ChangeTower
Rating: Beginner
Features:
- Monitor and track website changes
- Customize your tracking efforts

Monitor, track, and archive website changes. Compare visual, text, keyword, image and HTML change history. Get detailed alerts over email. They have free and premium versions for this tool. There are different features and steps you can do to start using it:

STEP 1: Monitor URL Web pages
Choose a URL to monitor for web page changes or set for archival. The engines will crawl and capture a full-page visual screenshot, text-based content snapshot, and source code.

ChangeTower's powerful monitoring network tracks changes to websites over time. They will notify you when it detects a change matching your settings, record, and archive a snapshot of your page automatically.

STEP 2: Create custom alerts
Select a part of the page to monitor for visual changes, or choose to monitor for keywords, sentences, code updates, images and more. Create advanced sets of criteria to monitor for. You decide what element(s) of a web page to monitor, and when to send you change alerts.

STEP 3: Get detailed reports
Filter, sort, and get detailed change reports with ease with ChangeTower's notification feed. Quickly locate the changes that matter most, reference and compare time-stamped web page snapshots. Track website changes whenever a matching change is detected. They'll show you exactly what changed and provide a detailed change report.

There are dozens of various features and benefits of using this tool. One of them is social media monitoring, where you can detect any change in real-time there. Take a look at this tool and enjoy using it.

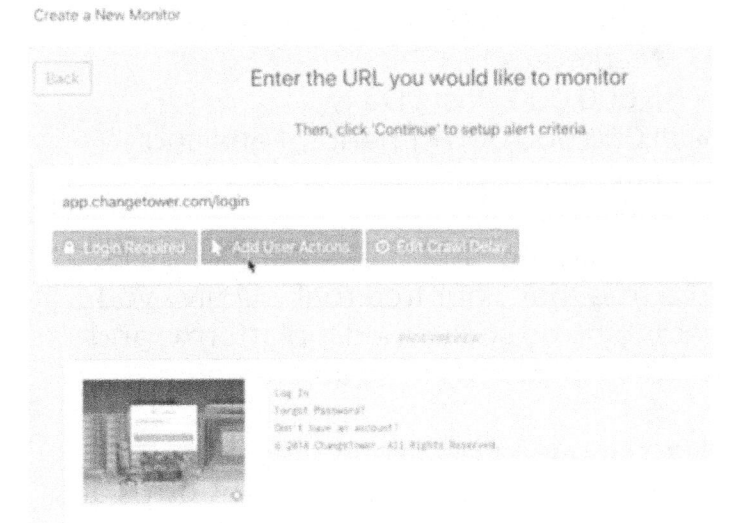

Dlvrit
Rating: Beginner
Features:
- Track social media posts and blogs all in one place

Put your social media on autopilot. Automatically schedule and post blogs, photos, RSS, news and videos to Facebook, Twitter, LinkedIn, Pinterest, Instagram and others. You can also use this tool to create candidates, clients, or competitors on various social media channels.

You can auto-share from anywhere. Auto-post items from RSS feeds, e-commerce sites, photo sharing apps, social networks and more. Powering social media success with:

- Around 1,750,000 Publishers and Marketers
- 5,000,000 Posts Daily
- 1,000,000,000+ Friends, Fans and Followers

This is a paid tool and there is an option to start a free trial. Your free trial will give you access to three social media platforms and three daily posts with 15 queued items.

Pick among your best matching ones according to your social media platforms and schedule your posts easily as never before.

Feedly

Rating: Beginner
Features:
- Organize trends

- Blogs and website news
- Manage everything within the extension tool

Your central place to organize, read, and share the information you need to stay ahead of the next big trend in your industry. This one's more for staying up to date on blogs and website news.

Feedly is a news aggregator application for various web browsers and mobile devices running iOS and Android. It is also available as a cloud-based service.
It compiles news feeds from a variety of online sources for the user to customize and share with others.

1. Organize and read all your trusted publications and blogs in one place

2. Train Leo, your AI research assistant, to read your feeds and filter out the noise

3. Collaboratively research and share key industry trends

Feedly is a secure space where you can privately organize and research the topics and trends that matter to you

Feedly is funded by the community that uses it. This means that you can focus on optimizing your time instead of creating a feed that mines your attention.

You can start using this tool in three steps. Just sign up for a free account and do the following:
1. Find and organize the right sources
2. Train Leo to filter out the noise
3. Share insights with your team

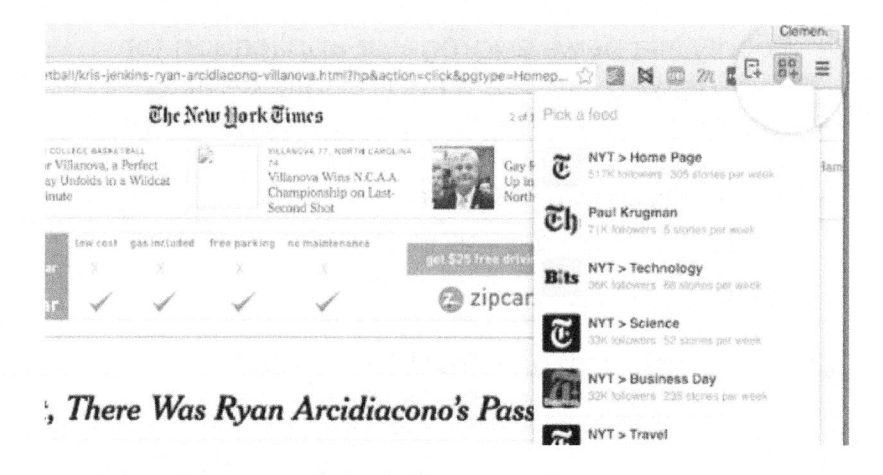

Indeed Resume
Rating: Beginner
Features:
- The biggest database on earth
- Target potential candidates with specific research criteria
- Cons: you will get blocked from seeing full names without having a paid subscription

Create a free email newsletter based on your search criteria.

Reach out and introduce yourself. The Indeed talent database has more than 120 million resumes. Find candidates across every industry and location. Target your search by education, title, location, company, skills and experience.

More than five million resumes added or updated every month. Sign up for Resume Alerts to receive new resumes. The process is simple, just follow the steps there.

Find an interesting candidate. Reach out and send a message directly from Indeed Resume. Start with using it in just a few steps. Go to the official website and sign up for a free account. Next, you can enjoy the resume researching for the potential candidates.

LinkedIn Sales navigator or Recruiter
Rating: Advanced
Features:
- Track and manage updates on candidate profiles
- CRM Project Features
- Message a large pool of candidates
- Manage leads through the whole process

You can "star" profiles in LinkedIn Recruiter. Any updates on the profile will be sent right to your email address. If you save your search strings – they will also recommend updated user profiles on a weekly basis.

It is an all-encompassing hiring platform for talent professionals that helps find, connect with, and manage the people you want to be on your team.

Find the right people fast. Cut down your hiring time with access to the world's largest professional network. You'll get up-to-date insights on more than 690 million members, advanced search filters, and recommended matches to prioritize based on who is most open to hearing from you.

Once you've got your shortlist of candidates, connect with them using personalized InMail even if you don't have their contact information. Bulk messaging and saved templates let you reach out to more candidates even faster.

Easily share candidate profiles with hiring managers (with or without Recruiter access) for feedback. You can also tag your teammates, see your teammates' communication history with candidates, and track the performance of your InMails.

You can use this tool in certain steps:

1. Search for any candidate on LinkedIn using keyword search, Boolean search, and 20+ advanced search filters.

2. Narrow in on people who are more likely to respond: Those who've indicated they're open to new opportunities or those who've engaged with your brand on LinkedIn.

3. Contact any candidate on LinkedIn with Recruiter's messaging tool, InMail. You get 150 InMail messages per month per team member.

4. Easily and collaboratively manage your pipeline with powerful collaboration and analytics tools.

Spoonbill.io
Rating: Beginner
Features:
- Receive weekly updates on changes
- Track a large pool of leads quickly

Spoonbill is a fun tool for tracking profile changes of the people you follow on Twitter. This is an awesome tool for finding the right people on your Twitter profile and using it will take only one click.

How it works:
1. First, you sign up.
2. Then Spoonbill looks at all the folks you're following on Twitter.

3. They will check every couple minutes to see if they've changed their profile information.
4. If they have, they record it!
5. Then, every morning (or every week), Spoonbill will send you an email with all the changes.

It's simple like that. Using this tool is such a pleasure if you are focused on Twitter and recruiting there.

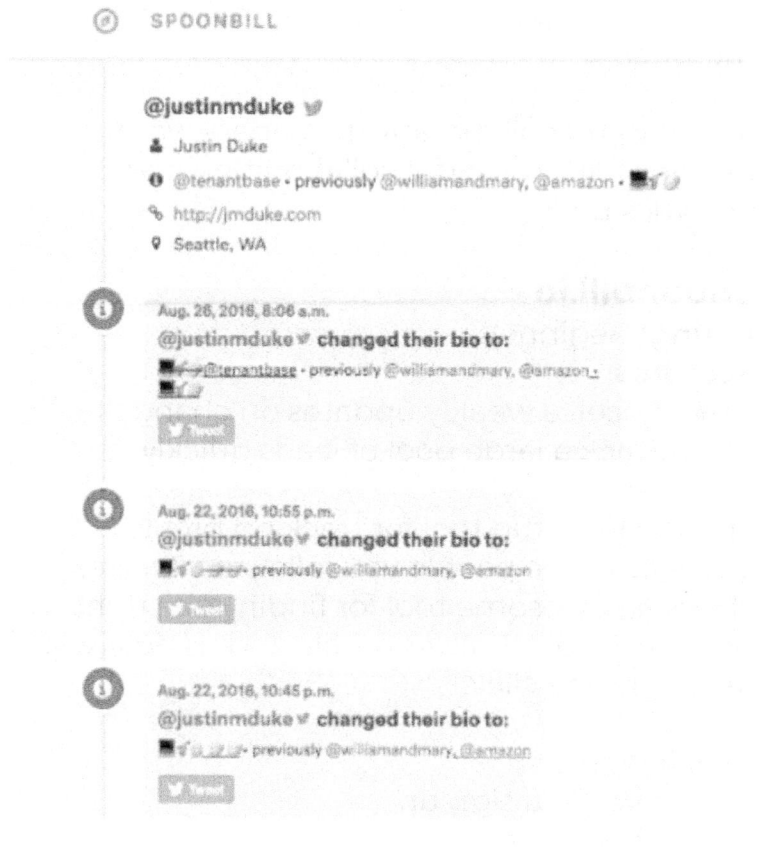

Talkwaker
Rating: Advanced
Features:
- Powerful analytics
- Track leads quickly
- Influencer marketing features

Talkwalker is an incredibly powerful social media analytics tool and social media monitoring tool recommended by brands and agencies worldwide. It's a paid resource but comes highly recommended by our sourcing community.

You will get social insights for the world's most impactful brands. Go from intelligence to impact.

Talkwalker is your extra set of eyes and ears. Its AI-powered analysis provides real-time insights into what's happening on all social channels and online media across 187 languages. This enables you to quickly identify issues and complaints before a crisis hits.

Your social media presence is paramount. Measure its impact. Benchmark your brand and campaigns with the tools proven KPI frameworks. Measure sentiment and brand health.

Connect social efforts to real business results and provide your management with instant reports. Compare your results to the competition across every channel. Discover what customers really think about your brands and products in real-time.

Maximize the social performance of your communication campaigns with data-driven technology. Find the best stories and the true influencers to boost your brand power.

With Quick Search, spot the trending stories on your brand and industry in real-time. Amplify your brand message for one global impact.

This tool costs $9000 per year with dozens of features and marketing insights. Using this tool is such an amazing experience if you are focused on social media marketing for business purposes.

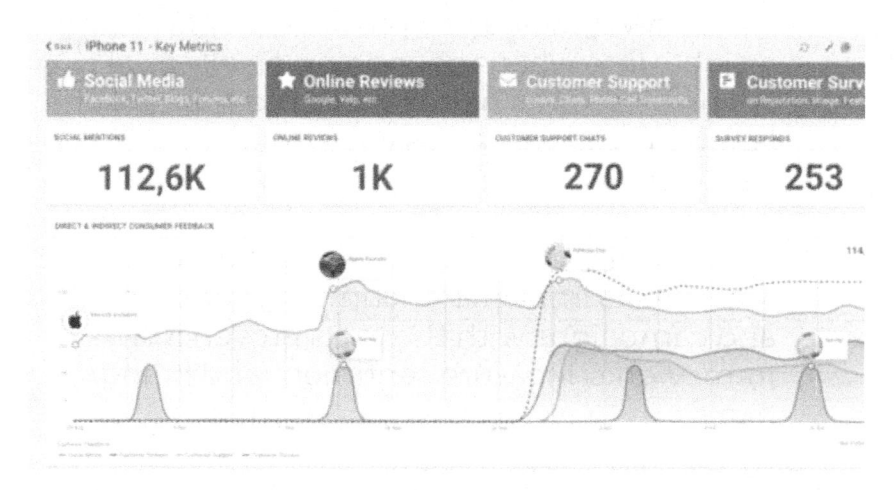

Versionista
Rating: Beginner
Features:
- Monitor HTML pages online, including PDFs
- Detect changes on any web or social profile page

It's a free way to monitor and track website page changes. Detecting changes to web page updates. Get immediate website change alerts over email.

Website Change Tracking at Scale:
- Monitor changes to HTML, PDFs, dynamic content
- Auto-crawl and monitor changes across entire sites
- Cloud-based solution with non-stop support
- Simple, powerful filters to screen irrelevant changes
- Color-coded comparisons show deletions, additions
- Detailed email summaries and instant change alert

Web Change Intelligence for Business:
- Thousands of brands trust us to watch website changes

- Regulatory intelligence and compliance automation
- Invite your team and collaborate
- Workflow management and team coordination
- Built for compliance, procurement, SEO, and more
- Download a shareable PDF about Versionista

Using it is a simple process and there are six subscription plans starting at $19 per month.

Monitor Website Changes.
Track Web Page Edits.
Change Detection & Alerts For Entire Sites.

crawlm

Monitor For Changes

Visualping
Rating: Beginner
Features:
- Tracking changes on the web
- Get real-time notifications

Visualping is the easiest to use website checker, webpage change monitoring, and website change detector.

They provide simple yet powerful change analytics. More than 1.5 million people use Visualping to be alerted for changes.

You can set up a change alert in less than one minute. Use the bulk import function for multiple pages. Here is the process:

1. Choose a page to monitor and click go
2. Select the area to track (or the whole page)
3. Chose how much change you want to be alerted for
4. Select the frequency of checks
5. Input the email where receive the alerts

Eighty-three percent of Fortune 500 companies use Visualping; there are more than 10,000 companies which have a group plan, so keep in mind that this is a powerful business tool for tracking changes on the web.

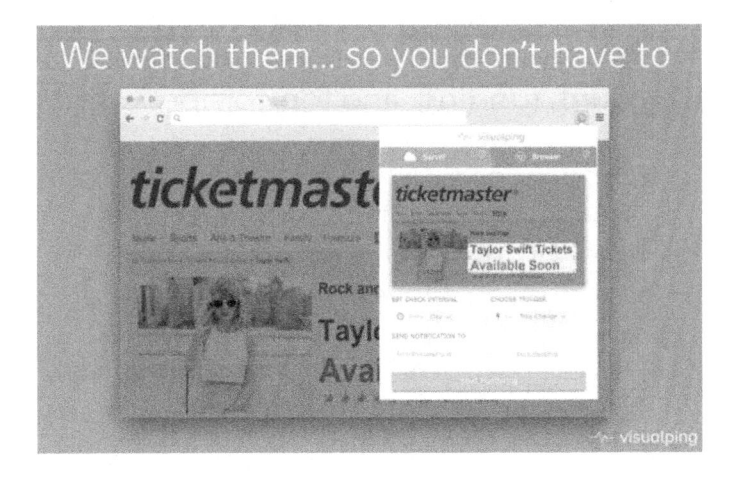

Owler Alerts
Rating: Beginner
Features:
- Multiple platforms social media integration
- Real-time insights and alerts
- Research and track all the companies worldwide

Owler is the world's largest community-based competitive insights platform that provides real-time news, alerts and company insights to help you win. I mostly use this tool to find other company competitors.

Track the companies that matter to you. Hard-to-find company data and strategic news alerts for savvy executives, marketers, and sales professionals.

1. Access exclusive information on over 13 million public and private businesses, including annual revenue, employee count, funding, and top competitors.

2. Discover companies that could boost your business with Advanced Search. Filter by industry, sector, geography, revenue, employee count, and more.

3. Filter a real-time feed of the latest news to uncover events that could move your

business forward, including funding, layoffs, and more.

4. Follow the companies that matter to you to receive daily news updates and customize real-time push news alerts for over 16 event types.

Owler offers exclusive options for teams, including custom keyword alerts, Salesforce integration, brand customization, specialized training for your sales team, and API integrations.

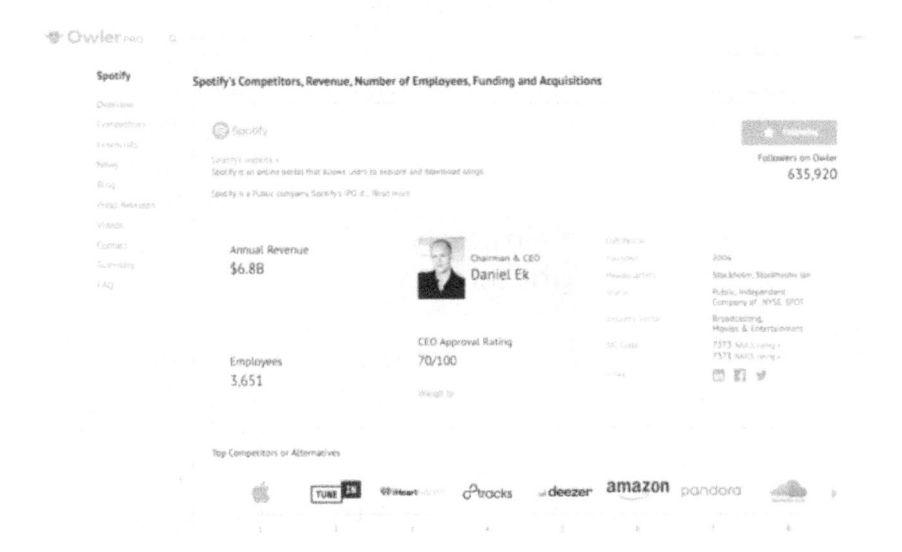

Google Alerts
Rating: Beginner
Features:
- Fast searching for prospects

- Get notifications on any updates from websites or posts online
- Use this to monitor your competition, clients, or candidates online

Need a way to monitor and multitask your daily searches? Google Alerts may be the right solution for you!

Basically, you can subscribe to your keyword search directly on Google. As soon as something new gets posted online, you will receive an update directly in your email inbox. This simple yet useful trick has helped me find active candidates as well as finding client leads.

Google Alerts will help you automate the search process and help you reach out to the right prospects faster. It will cut back on your time searching aimlessly online and help you focus on the right targets.

Simply log into Google Alerts and include a Boolean string. After this, go to advanced features. I recommend selecting the following: at most once a week, web sources within the United States, and only see the best results.

Here are ways to use Google Alerts:

Searching for Active Candidates

Searching for published resumes:
(intitle:resume OR inurl:resume) (skill set) ("saint paul" OR 55110)

Searching for companies with layoff news (Select News as the Source)
For example:

layoffs * "Target.com"
("layoffs" OR "downsizing" OR "outsourcing") (company)

Searching for Client Prospects
Recently posted job positions based on locations. Search a niche skill set and add a location.
For example: "sitecore developer" ("minneapolis" OR "55111") -templates job jobs

Here's some other search phrases you can use:

("job opening" OR "job listing")

("hiring" OR "now hiring")

("career opportunity" OR "career opportunities")

Finding clients based off niche skill sets:
Maybe you've networked with every top java developer in Minneapolis? You can create different alerts to see when a company is

actively looking to fill a role. Try using these search phrases and include that niche skill set.

"send an updated resume to"
"send a resume to"
"email your resume"
"forward a resume"
"email your cv"
"send your cv"
"your resume to me at"

Monitoring Competitors
Subscribe to Google jobs – any time a new job is posted, you will receive an alert. You can use this to keep an eye on your competitor's job openings.

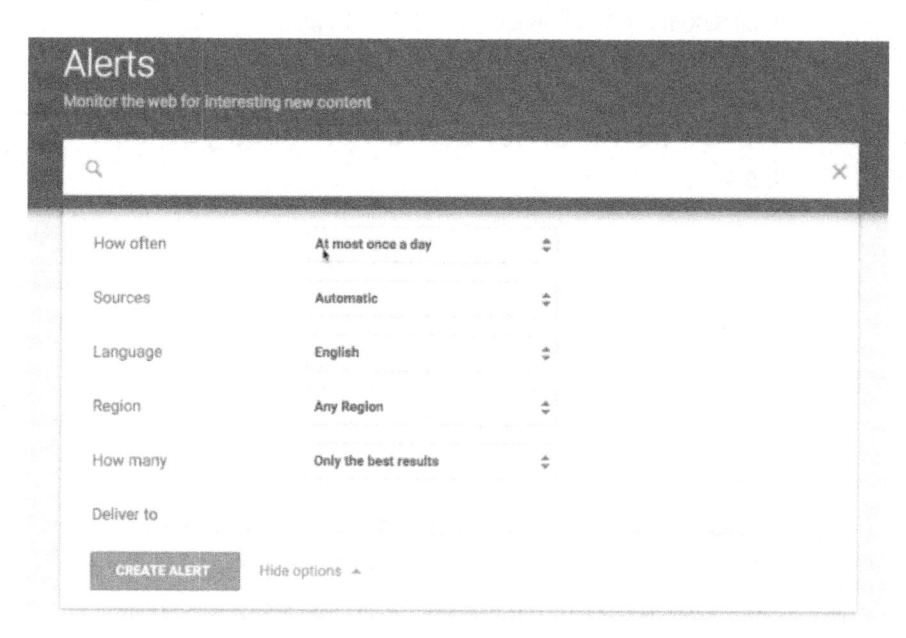

230

Chapter 14: Writing Tools

In this chapter, we will talk about different writing tools you can use for your business purposes. Let's dive in!

Why Do You Need Writing Tools?
Writing unbiased job descriptions is an absolute must for any recruiter. In order to attract the best and brightest for your company, you will need to craft a job description that is non-biased and SEO optimized. Thankfully, there's a ton of augment writing tools that a recruiter can use to write better job descriptions.

Grammarly
Rating: Beginner
Features:
- Best and most popular text error detector
- Plagiarism detector
- Simple extension plugin tool

Grammarly is an American-based technology company that offers a digital writing assistance tool based on artificial intelligence and natural language processing. The software was first released in July 2009 in Kyiv, Ukraine.

Compose bold, clear, mistake-free writing with Grammarly's AI-powered writing assistant. It works where you do. Get corrections from

Grammarly while you write on Gmail, Twitter, LinkedIn, and all other favorite sites.

From grammar and spelling to style and tone. Grammarly helps you eliminate errors and find the perfect words to express yourself. Grammarly allows you to get those communications out and feel confident, putting your best foot forward. Grammarly is like a little superpower, especially when you need to be at 110 percent.

This is a free tool, and you can use it as a Chrome extension as well. You just need to insert the text and the wrong grammar and spelling will be detected with red color. Also, if you buy the advanced version, you can detect any plagiarism from the web.

Textio
Rating: Beginner
Features:

- Employer's option writing better job descriptions
- Powerful language insights
- Branded content

Textio is made for a number of uses, and one of the most popular is to help employees find better words to attract the right people. It will predict how the things you write will help you attract talent and make suggestions to help you find better qualified and more diverse candidates.

Ultimately, it will cut down the time you spend writing and the Textio Score will help you predict how well the description will perform in the current job market.

When you're building a culture of belonging, every word counts. Textio brings the world's most advanced language insights into your hiring and employer brand content every time you write.

There are different features:

1. Use the tool to optimize your job description to attract diverse applicants to your openings.
2. To reach the best candidates, successful talent leaders are creating world-class employer brands. It all begins with how you sound.

3. Building a culture of inclusion takes more than just a good EOE statement. Infuse all of your talent content with the language of belonging.
4. Data insights have transformed every aspect of work, except the words we use every single day. Bring predictive analytics to the language of business.

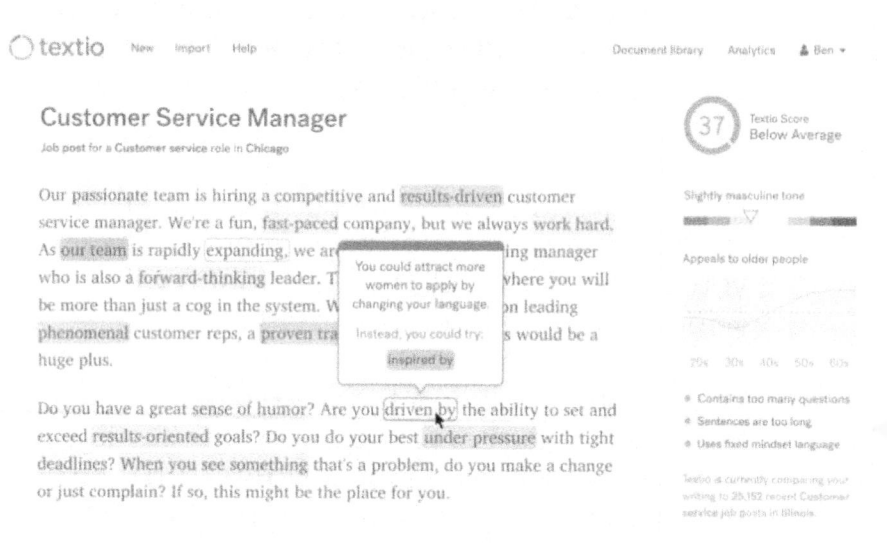

GlossaryTech

Rating: Beginner
Features:
- Easily define any technical skilled term
- Understand advanced tech terms within seconds

Learn tech terms while reading resumes, web sourcing, or just browsing – no more copy and pasting into Google to find out what a technology does.

There are different categories you can search for:
- Technologies
- Quality Assurance (QA)
- Game Development
- Software Infrastructure (DevOps)
- Web Design
- Product Management
- Project Management
- Leadership
- Development Methodologies
- Software Architecture
- Fundamental Programming Concepts
- Programming Paradigms
- Data Science
- Roles in Software Development
- Embedded
- Cloud Computing
- Cyber Security

Here's what the extension offers
- Highlights technical terms on a web page.
- Provides short, concise definitions for all the technical terms listed alongside alternatives/related terms.
- Allows you to filter all found terms by category (Front-end, Back-end, QA, etc.). Each category has its own color.

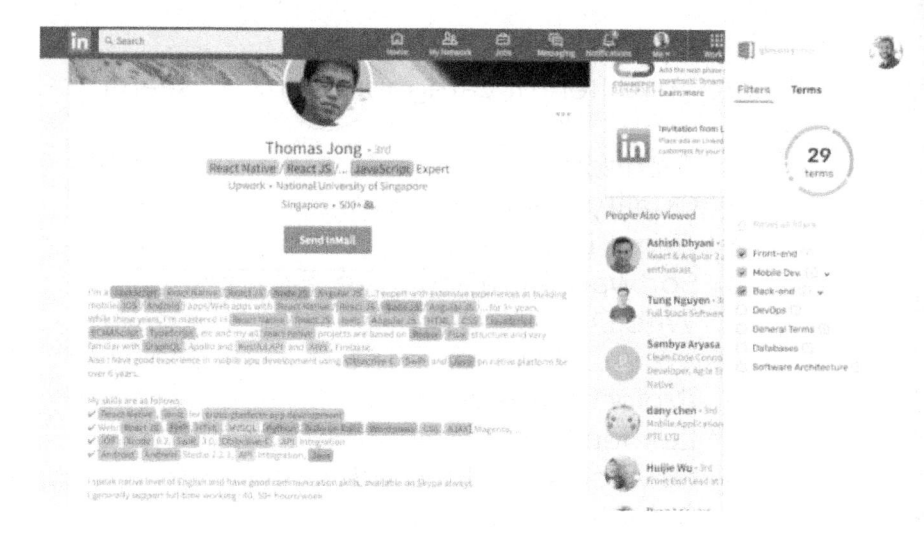

Joblint

Rating: Beginner
Features:

- Free tool that decodes your job descriptions
- Suggest alternative words to help attract diverse applicants

Allows you to test tech job posts for issues with sexism, culture, expectations, and recruiter fails. Keywords like Ninja, Go-Getter, or other terms can be a turn off to diverse candidates. This tool helps analyze your current openings and gives you suggestions on how to improve it.

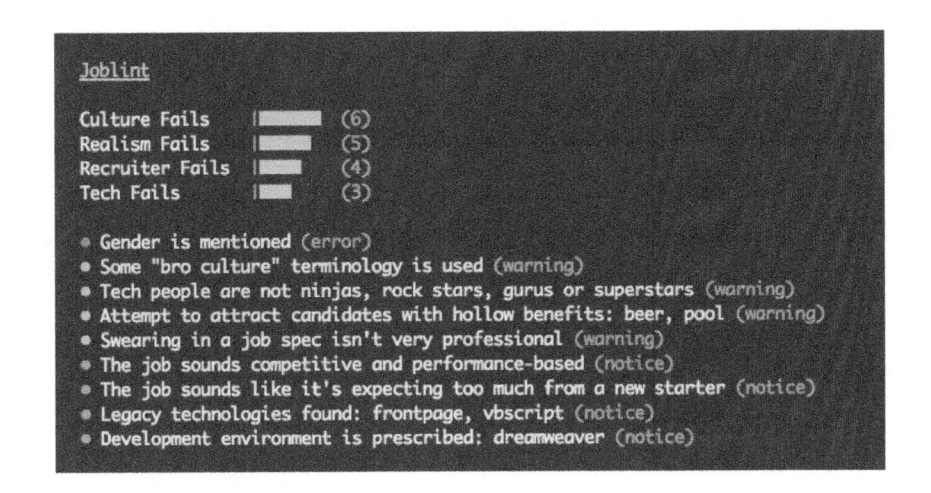

```
Joblint

Culture Fails   ▮▮▮   (6)
Realism Fails   ▮▮▮   (5)
Recruiter Fails ▮▮    (4)
Tech Fails      ▮▮    (3)

• Gender is mentioned (error)
• Some "bro culture" terminology is used (warning)
• Tech people are not ninjas, rock stars, gurus or superstars (warning)
• Attempt to attract candidates with hollow benefits: beer, pool (warning)
• Swearing in a job spec isn't very professional (warning)
• The job sounds competitive and performance-based (notice)
• The job sounds like it's expecting too much from a new starter (notice)
• Legacy technologies found: frontpage, vbscript (notice)
• Development environment is prescribed: dreamweaver (notice)
```

Gender Decoder

Rating: Beginner
Features:
- Removes masculine-coded language
- Gender and diversity focused terms suggestions
- Job description SEO optimization

Without realizing it, we all use language that is subtly "gender-coded." Society has certain expectations of what men and women are like and how they differ and this seeps into the language we use. Think about "bossy" and "feisty": we almost never use these words to describe men.

This linguistic gender-coding show up in job adverts as well, and research has shown that it puts women off applying for jobs that are advertised with masculine-coded language.

This site is a quick way to check whether a job advert has the kind of subtle linguistic gender-coding that has this discouraging effect.

Gender Decoder for Job Ads

Without realising it, we all use language that is subtly 'gender-coded'. Society has certain expectations of what men and women are like, and how they differ, and this seeps into the language we use. Think about "bossy" and "feisty": we almost never use these words to describe men.

This linguistic gender-coding shows up in job adverts as well, and research has shown that it puts women off applying for jobs that are advertised with masculine-coded language.*

This site is a quick way to check whether a job advert has the kind of subtle linguistic gender-coding that has this discouraging effect. Find out more about how this works.

Paste your job ad here

Text Analyzer
Rating: Beginner
Features:
- Submit up to 10,000 words
- Analyze job descriptions with ease

Free software utility which allows you to find the most frequent phrases and frequencies of words. Non-English language texts are supported. It also counts number of words, characters, sentences, and syllables.

Simply copy and paste your text in the box above and click submit. You will get more accurate results for texts of over 50 or so words.

Each word in the submitted text is compared to a list of the 10,000 most commonly used English words. Based on each word's position on the list and the average word and sentence length, an algorithm is used to rate the difficulty of the text.

You can expect slightly different results compared to the Flesch-Kincaid index. The Flesch-Kincaid index mainly looks at sentence length and word length, whereas this tool focuses on the complexity of language.

TapRecruit
Rating: Beginner
Features:
- Optimize Job descriptions
- Rates and scores each of your job descriptions
- Suggest other terms to optimize job descriptions

TapRecruit offers a comprehensive recruiting analytics suite that helps you diagnose quality and diversity issues throughout your talent pipeline.

Measure your job performance with recruiting analytics. Write inclusive job descriptions with augmented writing.

TapRecruit's augmented writing platform is trusted by hiring teams from across the globe to improve the clarity and effectiveness of their job descriptions.

TapRecruit provides language guidance and, more importantly, content guidance via augmented writing so the hiring teams can write job descriptions that encourage qualified candidates to apply regardless of their gender, ethnicity, or background.

Create an inclusive process by avoiding biases such as Racism, Tokenism, Ableism, Ageism, Nationalism, Elitism, and Religion bias. With a robust recruiting analytics suite, TapRecruit's job description software helps your hiring teams diagnose quality and diversity issues throughout your talent pipeline.

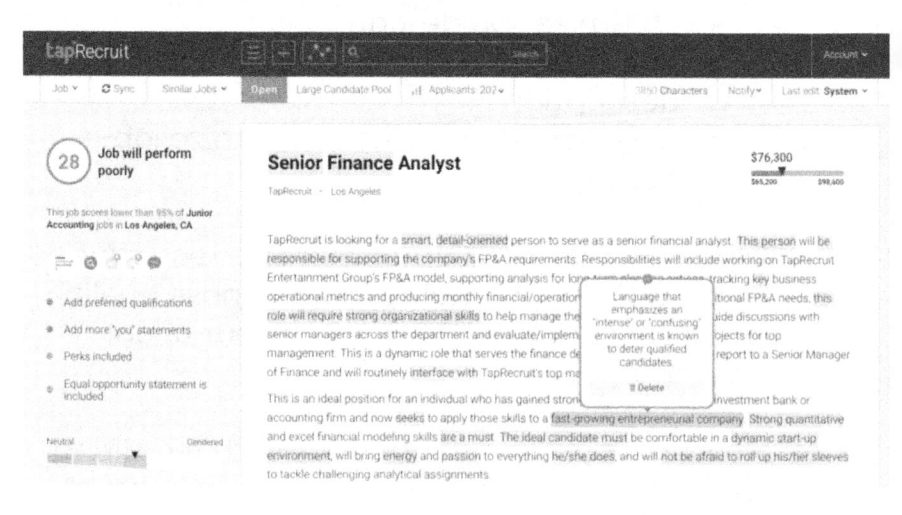

TalVista

Rating: Beginner
Features:
- Job description SEO optimization
- Real-time feedback

Improve your diversity recruiting. The TalVista conscious inclusion decision support platform helps users to be more aware of bias with data-driven hiring and view beyond the noise of unconscious bias.

Greater conscious inclusive decision making ensures a more diverse and inclusive talent pool and workforce. TalVista supports improved diversity recruiting and hiring in three ways:

1. Optimizing job descriptions
2. Blind CV and Resumes reviews
3. Structured interviewing

Scientific- and research-based data have been added to TalVista's proprietary algorithms to identify problematic words within job descriptions that can keep diverse candidates from applying for your posted jobs. With real-time feedback, you'll write more inclusive and effective job descriptions that attract male, female, and underrepresented candidates.

Name, gender, school, and other personal identifying information are redacted to help evaluators focus on what matters most for job success, core job criteria, rather than fixating on race, gender, or ethnicity.

Plan your interviews to focus on the best indicators of job success. Help interviewers focus on core job needs and criteria. Now it's easy for interviewers to conduct effective, objective, and professional interviews while being mindful and present with little prep time.

There are different tools you can use here and your recruiting process will be as effective as possible.

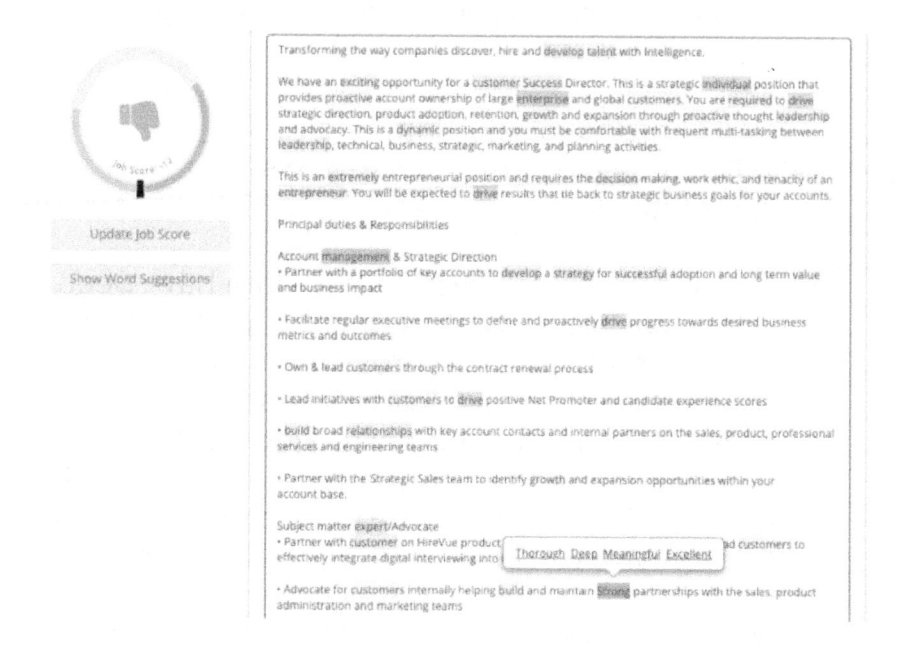

Applied
Rating: Beginner
Features:

- Quickly score your job description
- Gives suggestions on alternative words
- Optimizes the job descriptions SEO

Unbiased hiring is the future. Be part of the change. Blind hiring software that empowers teams to make hiring decisions based on data, with a process candidates love.

Biases lead us to make less-than-perfect hiring decisions, meaning the best candidates can fall through the cracks.

Applied turns inclusive recruitment into a science. By testing the real skills needed for each job, you can eliminate bias and find your ideal candidate.

Allow candidates to showcase their talent and give hiring teams real insights by testing for skills required for the job.

Incognito applications mean that you can make a judgement based on merit, revealing your top candidates based on their ability, not their background.

Get both live and historic pipeline data to optimize your hiring workflows and understand which sources give your organization the best-performing candidates. Using this tool, you can get access to diversity recruitment and candidate performance data for informed decisions on how to optimize your hiring process.

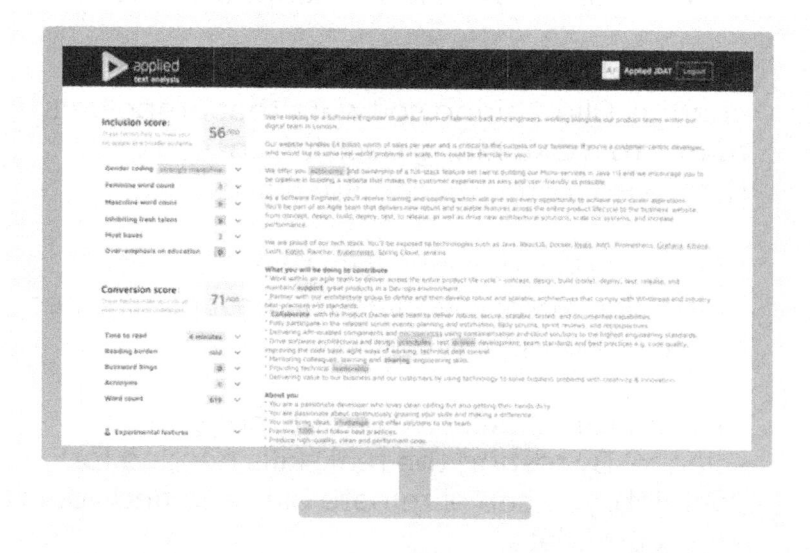

JobWriter.io
Rating: Beginner
Features:
- Helps write and optimize a job description

Forget the same dull copy that makes recruitment ads all sound alike. JobWriter enhanced postings don't just describe jobs; they tell your story about your goals, your organization's culture, and what it genuinely feels like to work in a particular job.

Candidates will know intrinsically if their personality makes them a natural fit. They'll also feel comfortable about the work environment and how their talents will be valued. And finally, they'll be able to see themselves aligned with your corporate culture.

Appealing to candidates on these three levels helps ensure that they share your expectations, values, and attitudes.

JobWriter postings are written to sound like they're talking to one person rather than everyone, and in a more human voice, the way people naturally speak – not corporate mumbo jumbo. The job postings are honest and authentic, making it easy for people to get excited about the opportunity.

In fact, with this novel approach, candidates know whether they'll be happy on the job. Interestingly, the same copy that woos candidates who share your vision dissuades those who don't. Obviously, this up-front self-screening helps you hire more efficiently. Not to mention, happy employees are more engaged, productive, and tend to stay longer.

With the click of a button, JobWriter will scan your posting, highlight words that should be changed to make it entirely gender neutral, and suggest alternatives.

Last but not least, JobWriter can take your standard diversity language and improve the attractiveness of your organization to diverse candidates on a job-by-job basis. With a single click on any particular job, JobWriter includes additional content for that role related to your focus on inclusiveness.

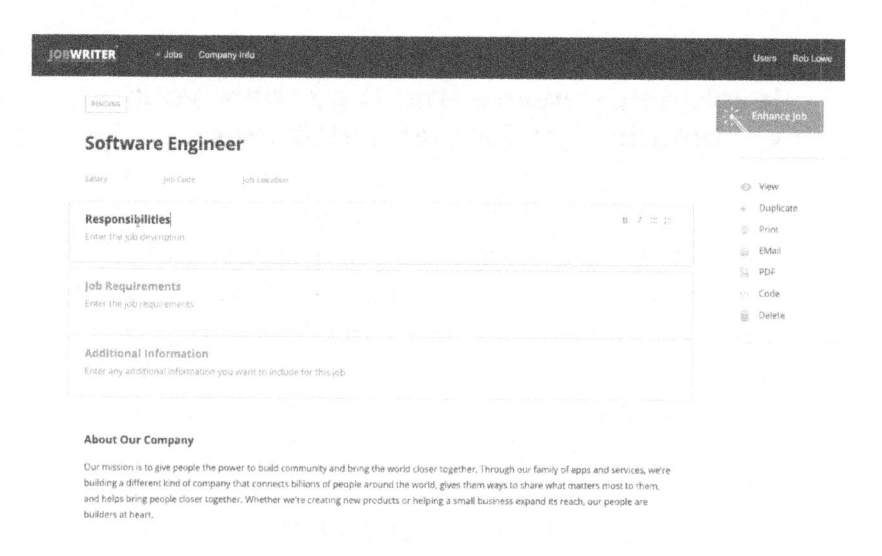

Chapter 15: Calendar Scheduling Tools

Do you feel like you could use a few extra hours in your day? This sentiment is shared by many, especially recruiters who are constantly juggling appointments and facing changing schedules from managers and clients. However, there is good news! There are now apps available to help manage your schedule and make life easier. Here are the top ten appointment scheduling apps currently available on the market, specifically designed to be of great use to recruiters

Acuity
Rating: Beginner
Features:
- Schedule your candidate's interview
- Easily link your calendar and sync it

This app can be a true timesaver for Recruiters. Instead of a few back-and-forth emails or calls, simply have the candidate schedule an open time. You can link your current calendar (Google, Outlook, or iCal) so the app automatically syncs with your schedule.

While there is a free trial, the best option to try out would be the $15 plan. This option sends reminder emails so your candidate won't forget about their appointment and includes an automatic time zone converter. If you are talking to candidates outside our time zone, this could avoid all the missed calls due to confusion.

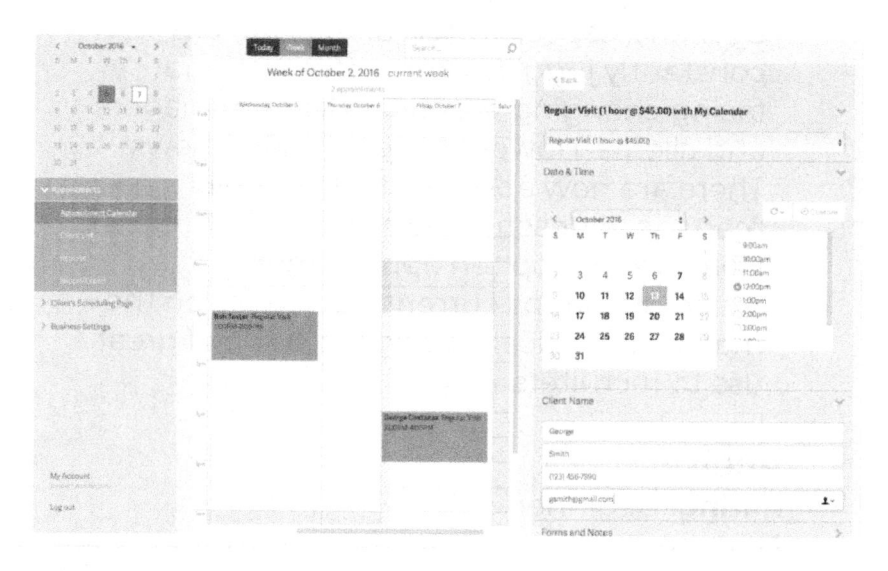

Calendly
Rating: Beginner
Features:
- Voted one of the best calendar apps tools in 2021
- Schedule your appointments
- Send notifications and follows ups

If simplicity is what you are after, Calendly is a fantastic option. Not only is it super simple to use, it can save you a ton of time. Recruiters who need to schedule interviews with hiring managers will want to sign up for the premium option to include them on the invites. At $8, it is about half the price of Acuity.

According to their sales page, Calendly can speed up the recruiting process by simplifying the scheduling process. If you aren't sure if it's worth the eight bucks, there is a free trial to try it out.

Gigabook
Rating: Beginner
Features:
- Optimized in different devices
- Effective and fast scheduling

Detail-oriented Recruiters may prefer a system like Gigabook for their scheduling needs. They offer event tickets and group planning that would come in handy for recruiting events.

There is a to-do list feature to help you keep track of everything you need to get done, as well as the standard options like appointment reminders. I like the reporting feature, which could be helpful if you want to analyze your data. Pricing for this service starts at $7 a month and also offers a free trial.

On the other hand, Gigabook is an online appointment scheduling platform that helps businesses schedule clients for activities, send reminders, and take payments. Their motto is "Here is a better way to run your business." This tool will help you:

- Stop Missing Opportunities
- Have Easy Access Means More Business
- Save Time and Money
- Improve Overall Client Experience
- Reduce No-Shows with Reminders
- Take Payments Online
- Manage Your Business from Anywhere

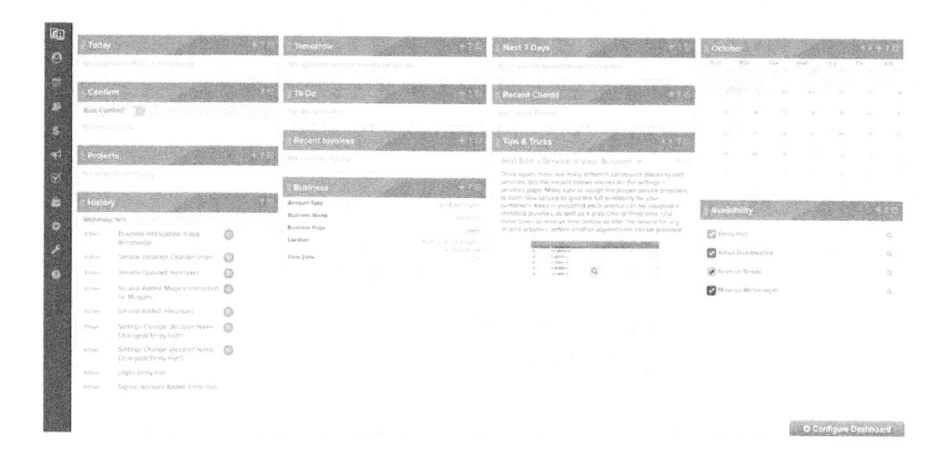

MyTime

Rating: Beginner

Features:
- Cloud based tool
- Marketing and recruiting features built in

Marketing is huge in the recruiting game, and MyTime integrated marketing into their app. If you want to run a campaign to try and gain interest for a hard to fill role, this may be the best option for you. Along with the marketing, the feature comes at a higher price tag, with the lowest option being $74 per month.

MyTime is as customizable as you need it to be and fully integrated. You can focus on customer experience instead of technology. MyTime is the leading cloud-based appointment scheduling, point of sale, and customer engagement solution for enterprise businesses which need to win in an omnichannel world.

Sign up for a free account and start using it for your business purposes.

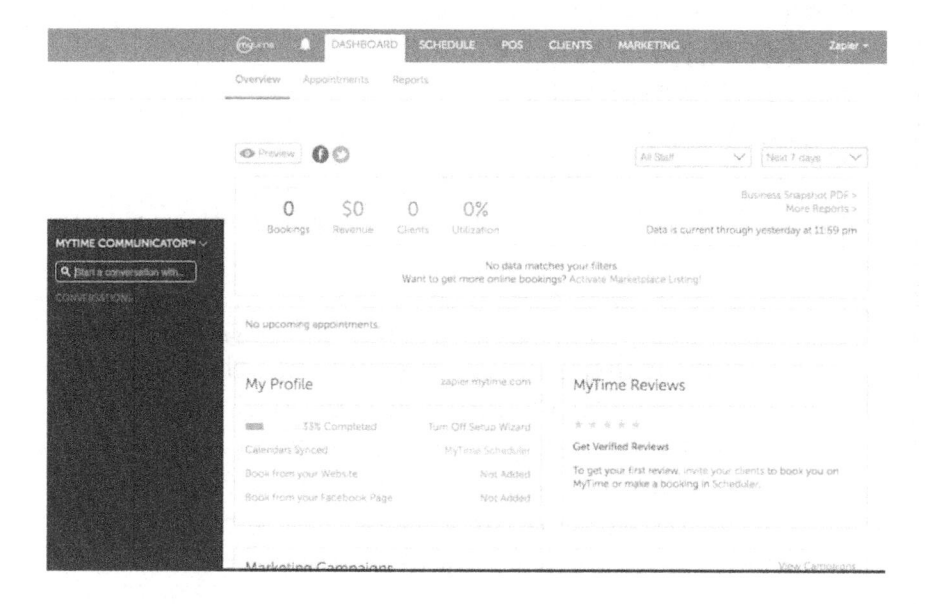

Setmore

Rating: Beginner
Features:

- Integration within different platforms
- Organize payments, bookings, and reminders

Does simple and free sound like the perfect option? Setmore is a great choice if you are on a budget. The app even allows you to store candidate information and send reminders to your candidates. While it may not have some of the features of the other apps, it lets you do a lot for the price tag!

Organize your business with 24/7 automated online booking, reminders, payments, and more. Manage all appointments through one online calendar planner to help your business run like clockwork.

There are different things you can benefit from:

1. Forget about chasing invoices and accept payments easily and securely online.

2. Add video meeting links to your appointments with Zoom or free Teleport integrations.

3. Customize your virtual office with personalized page URLs, logos, colors and more.

4. Integrate your Setmore calendar with your favorite apps for seamless scheduling.

Every interaction with a lead is an opportunity. Keeps your calendar scheduling software on-brand and bookings on target.

- Create your custom-branded URL
- Add your own logos and brand visuals
- Integrate with your website, Facebook, and Instagram

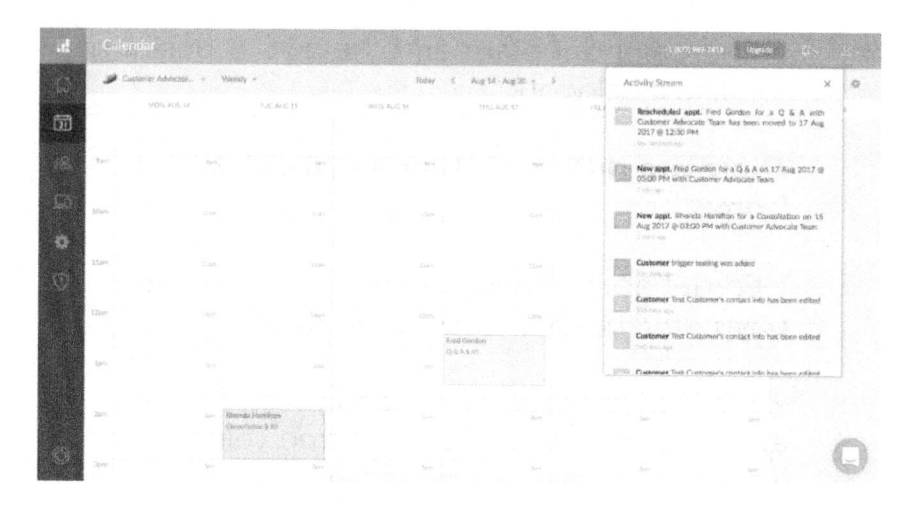

YouCanBook.me
Rating: Beginner
Features:
- Scheduling Automated
- Reminders and notification features

YouCanBook.me is another great option if you are looking for simplicity. Features include reminders, time zone conversion, and booking based on your calendar availability. If your company has specific branding they want to include, there is also an option to integrate those aspects.

If you are working with hiring managers, this is another great app that allows you to include their schedule as well. This reduces the time you have to spend coordinating several schedules. They offer a free account with basic features, or you can upgrade to the $10 a month plan for advanced features.

Connect with your calendar and only share the times you want with your customers – they book straight into your calendar. Customers get their own notifications, reminders, calendar invites, and more.

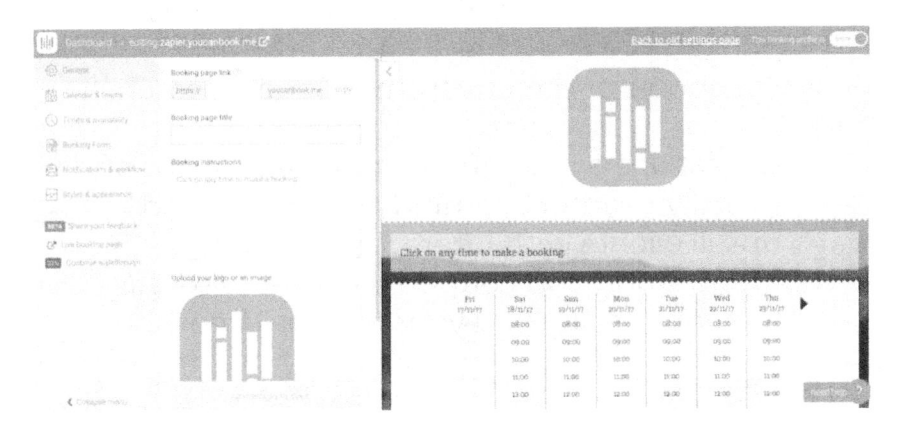

Vcita
Rating: Beginner
Features:
- CRM and scheduling
- Effective tracking
- Integration in social media

Vcita is an all-in option, giving you a CRM as well as a scheduling tool. If you don't have an applicant tracking system or it isn't giving you what you need, this could be a good replacement. You can have candidates scheduled online as with the other apps.

This app also includes features like lead capturing, a business page, and email campaigns. There is a free plan, but to get the benefits the $15 plan is the lowest option worth considering.

Build lasting relationships with client cards that guarantee you never forget a name, a face, or an opportunity. Get your services booked in a snap from your website, Facebook, or directly from a Google search.

Collect like a pro with actionable invoices and friendly payment reminders. Engage and upsell clients with interactive widgets, promotions, and coupons. You can use this tool for free starting your trial for 14 days.

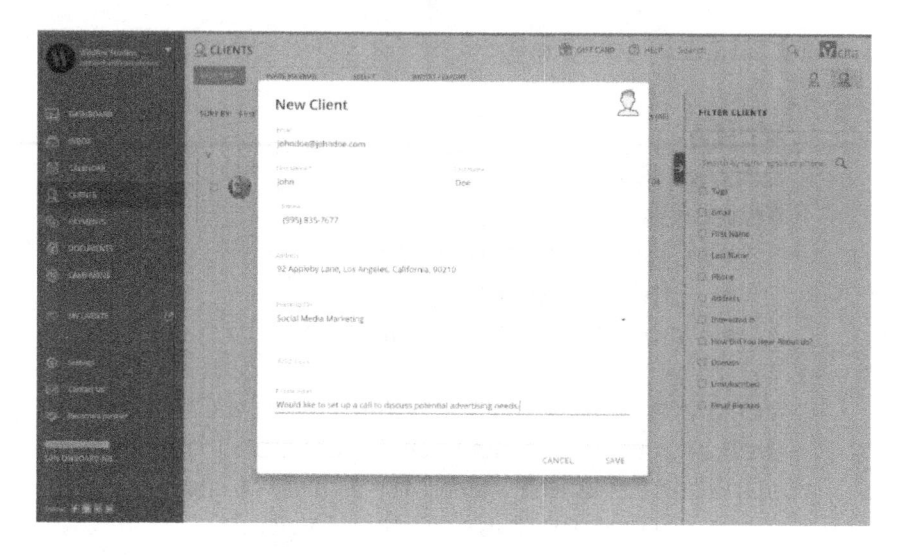

10to8
Rating: Beginner
Features:
- Zoom and Teams integration

- SMS text reminders

Targeting millennials with your recruiting efforts? The company, 10to8, offers SMS text messaging reminders for appointments, which in today's world is an amazing feature. It is included in the free plan, as well as 100 appointments per month. If you feel like you need to have more flexibility and support you can try the higher plans for 30 days for free. Schedule and run virtual appointments smoothly with 10to8 and make your business fully remote! Their native Zoom Video Conferencing and Microsoft Teams integrations enable you to host video appointments of all kinds, be it internal staff meetings, online classes, or remote medical appointments.

You can use this tool for free but there are three other paid packages with different features.

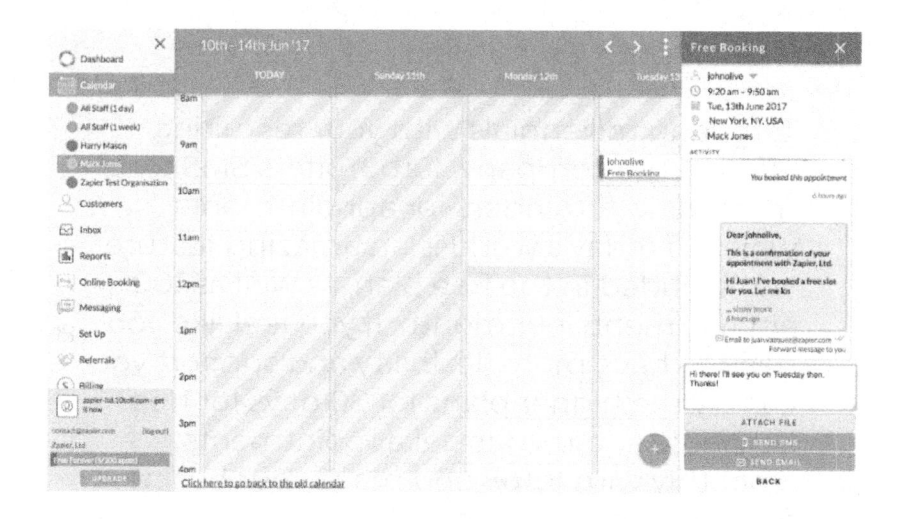

Appointlet

Rating: Beginner
Features:

- Effective scheduling and calendar integration
- Can see the whole teams' calendars
- Time zone reminders

Appointlet offers reminders, calendar integration, and even social media integration. Like many of the other apps listed, it automatically converts time zones and offers reminders for your candidates.
They have a lot of features that are included with every plan, including support and unlimited bookings. The lowest plan is $14 a month, but if you want the ability to include your managers in scheduling, you will need to opt for the $45 monthly option.

What you can do with this tool:

- Customize your appointment schedule and booking page.

- Share your personal booking page with your customers and prospects. You can integrate your scheduling page into your website, emails and landing pages.

- Your customers and prospects book an available time with you. It's automatically added to your calendar and theirs without the tedious back and forth.

I S T A R
CONSULTING

Schedule a meeting with the team

① Services ② Members ③ Times ④ Information ⑤ Review

The below times are available for booking

Times displayed in: US/Eastern

📅 Oct 8, 2015 - Oct 15, 2015 ⌄

Thu 10/8	Fri 10/9	Mon 10/12	Tue 10/13	Wed 10/14	Thu 10/15
9:00 AM	9:00 AM	10:00 AM	10:00 AM	9:30 AM	9:30 AM
9:30 AM	12:00 PM	10:30 AM	12:00 PM	10:00 AM	10:00 AM
10:00 AM	12:30 PM	11:00 AM	12:30 PM	10:30 AM	10:30 AM
10:30 AM	1:00 PM	11:30 AM	1:00 PM	11:00 AM	11:00 AM
3:00 PM	1:30 PM	12:00 PM	1:30 PM	11:30 AM	11:30 AM
3:30 PM	2:00 PM	12:30 PM	2:00 PM	12:00 PM	12:00 PM

ScheduleOnce

Rating: Beginner
Features:

- Cheaper in comparison with others
- Great organizing features
- Calendar integration with Gmail, Outlook, and others

This app is a great lower cost option offering unlimited booking on the basic $7 a month plan. It also includes reminders, time zone support, and calendar integration. While it does include SMS reminders, you have to purchase SMS credits.

If you use GoToMeeting for video interviews, you may want to consider the Professional plan at $15.80 per month which allows integration with the platform. ScheduleOnce also has a 15-day free trial if you want to test it before you sign up.

Recruiting is one of the most scheduling heavy jobs out there. To keep yourself organized and free up valuable time, adding one of the apps we mentioned in this article could be a lifesaver. Imagine all the additional candidates you could be speaking with if you weren't wasting time going back and forth on schedule? Increase your placements by trying an appointment scheduling app today.

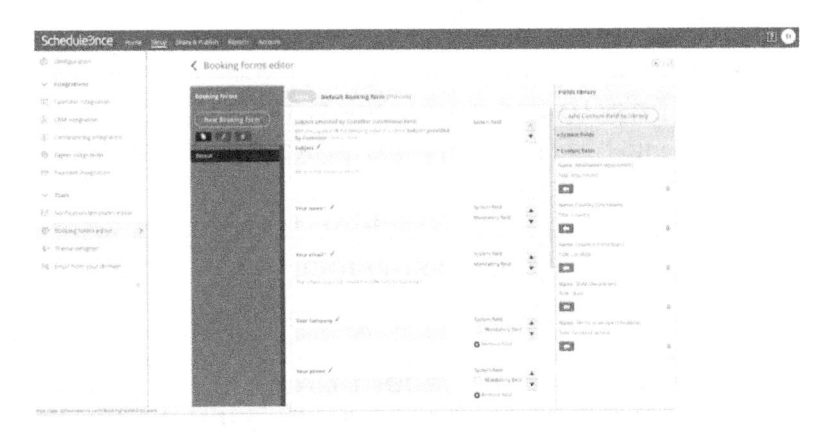

Chapter 16: Time Tracking Tools

In this chapter, we will discuss about different time tracking tools that you can use to track your employers' time and keep your workers on eye even if you collaborate online.

Why Do You Need Time Tracking Tools?
Time tracking is key to understanding how you spend your time, personally and in business. It is key to productivity, insight, and a healthy workflow. When you know which tasks take the most of your time, you can begin to reflect on whether that time is well spent.

Marinara Extension
Rating: Beginner
Features:
- Easy to use and track time
- Highly rated time managing Chrome extension
- Different time tracking features
- Use this tool to stay focused in timed increments

Pomodoro is an excellent time management assistant and it will help you with:

• Short and long breaks
• Toolbar icon with countdown timer
• Track Pomodoro history and stats

- Configurable long break intervals
- Configurable timer durations
- Desktop and tab notifications
- Audio notifications with over 20 sounds
- Ticking timer sounds
- Scheduled automatic timers

Workplace time management is a real challenge. Emails, texts, phone calls and even snack breaks prevent us from focusing on – and effectively executing – a single task at a time. For decades, countless people have used the Pomodoro technique to improve work and project productivity.

As working creatives, we found the Pomodoro method to be too rigid. Twenty-five-minute work segments with five- or 15-minute breaks are not ideal for all individuals, companies, or industries.

Reduce distractions, limit interruptions and complete tasks more efficiently with Marinara online productivity timer. The Pomodoro timer is a well-known productivity interval that has been shown to improve your productivity. It gives you a prescribed interval of 25 minutes of work, followed by a five-minute break. After four work intervals, there is a 15-minute break.

Marinara: Pomodoro Assistant

SETTINGS   HISTORY   FEEDBACK

Focus

Duration: 25 minutes

Timer sound:

   Stopwatch ▸ Hover to preview

   Speed: 240 beats per minute

When complete:

   ☑ Show desktop notification

actiTime

Rating: Beginner
Features:

- Integration in different browsers
- Sync with Trello and slack

actiTIME Timer is a great extension that works in Chrome to simplify the entire process of tracking your time. It's a robust tool and includes many features to help manage work and time spent on it. You can use it to track the number of hours you spend using different web apps and browsers and even count time spent working and then sync the report up with your actiTIME account.

That means, if someone was collaborating with Trello, they just need to start the timer when they open the app and then stop it when they're finished. The time record can be adjusted as necessary after the fact, but so long as you remember to start and stop the timer, you'll no longer have to rely on memory or constantly open a timesheet for immediate tracking.

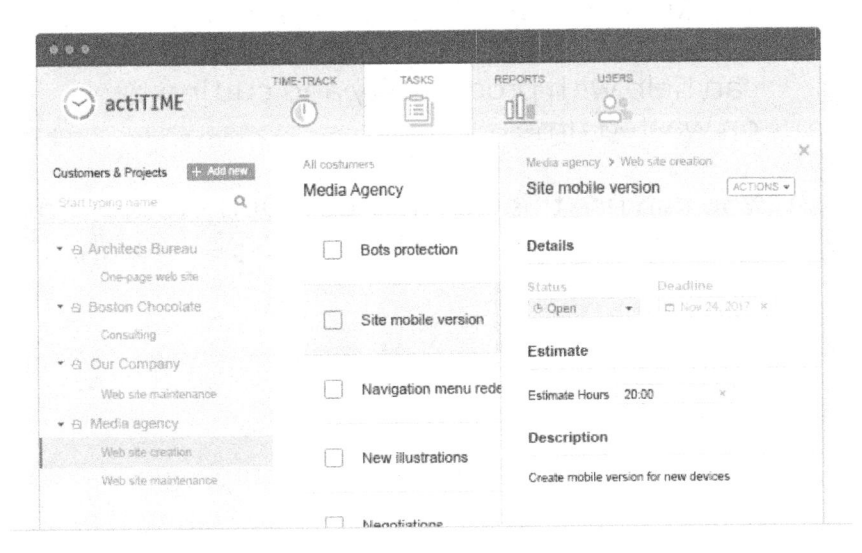

Tracking Time
Rating: Beginner
Features:
- Simple and easy to use
- Track your sourcing and searching efforts

TrackingTime is another extension that helps you to collect accurate information on how long it takes to get work done.

The data collected will be synced to the TrackingTime account for whoever is logged

265

in, allowing them to calculate the time they spent working and the total billable amount for that time. Plus, this extension makes reporting easy, even helping to understand how time is allocated among team members.

TrackingTime also has features to help you analyze the most time-intensive tasks, which can help with productivity and cutting back on wasted time.

You can use this tool for free, but there is a pro version which you can use for $5 per month.

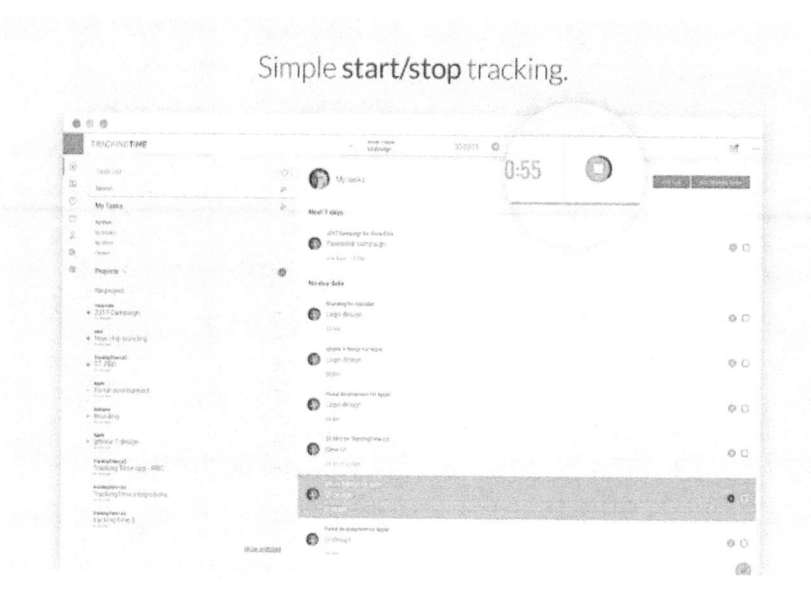

Simple **start/stop** tracking.

Elorus
Rating: Beginner
Features:
- Send invoices anywhere
- This is great for independent recruiters

- Tracking time according to data
- Monitor your team's productivity

The Elorus extension is part of a bigger online invoicing tool. Elorus tracks how much time you work and then calculates the total billable amount based on that data.

It also keeps track of the history of how you spend your time and you can use it for a whole team to monitor their performance and productivity over a certain period. It's excellent if you need billing features alongside time-tracking capabilities.

Generate professional and customized invoices in just a few steps. No matter the country, the currency, or the language of your client, they will handle it all.

- Send branded invoices to your clients
- Accept credit card payments for your invoices
- Save time with recurring invoices
- Set auto reminders for late payments

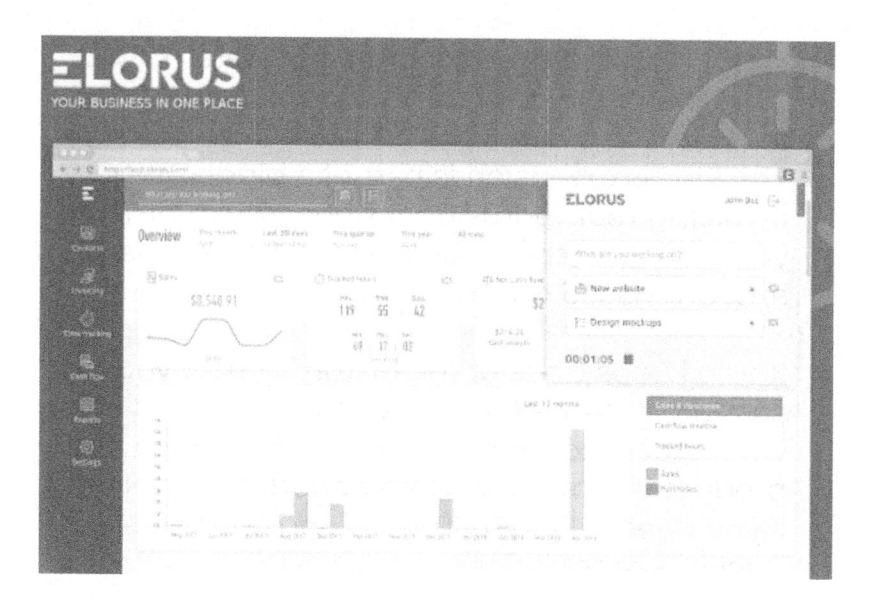

Clockify

Rating: Beginner
Features:
- Track your productivity
- Weekly updates
- Export data in PDF, CSV, or PDF documents

Last but not least on this list, Clockify is a timer extension that works as part of a larger time-tracking platform. It can help you improve your work performance by tracking your idle time and setting reminders for you. You can even use the built-in Pomodoro timer to help your productivity and focus, plus the work hour tracking means calculating invoices is easy. The automatic start/stop feature also helps increase accuracy.

Using this tool, you can:

1. Track hours using a timer
2. Log time in a timesheet
3. Categorize time by project
4. Mark time as billable
5. Visual time breakdown
6. Customizable reports
7. Share reports with others
8. Export as PDF, CSV, and Excel

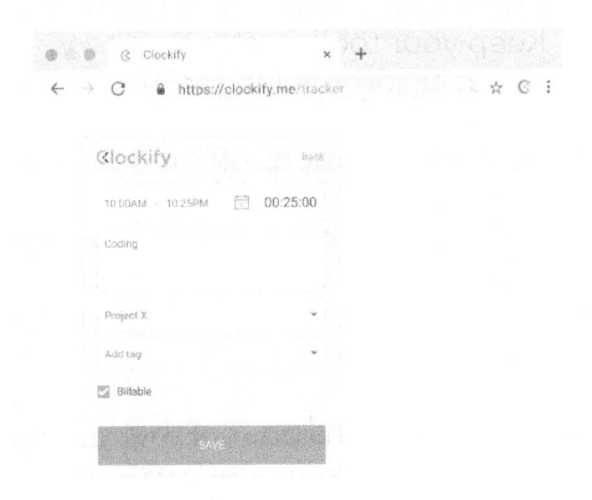

Chapter 17: Notable Mentions

These tools don't fit within the above chapter suggestions. I still wanted to highlight them in the final chapter of this book!

Extensity (Organization Extension)
Rating: Beginner
Features:
- Keep your browser fast – disable extensions you won't use right away
- Keep your toolbar clean
- An ideal companion for extensions collectors
- Turn all extensions off (and back on) with a single click
- Quick switch between several extensions groups using the Profiles feature
- Keep computers in sync with Chrome Cloud Storage support

Extensity is an extension tool that gives you quick access to all your active extensions and allows you to disable ones that you are not using. Basically, it's a simple one-page solution to manage all your extensions. You can set up different profiles to make it easy to simplify which extension at a given time. It's an exceptional extension that really helps improve my sourcing game.

It can solve memory and storage problems, improve your productivity, cut down on monotonous work, and probably save you 20-30 minutes a day doing things you didn't even realize ate up your time (like I did!). All the while, your computer will run more efficiently.

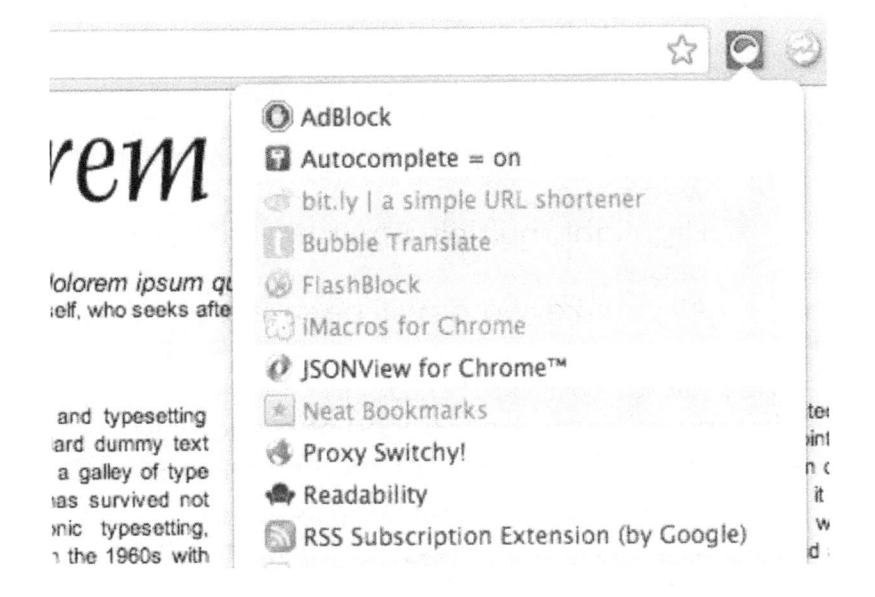

Multi-highlight Tool
Rating: Beginner
Features:
- Different platform integration
- Highlights keywords that you are sourcing for

As a Talent Sourcer in the tech space, I'm always looking for certain keywords on profiles. For example, I've been searching for Back End

Developers with Java, RESTful, spring, Hibernate, and Agile experience. When I'm viewing profiles on GitHub and Stack Overflow, I sometimes struggle with searching for every keyword. Thankfully, there's a browser extension called Multi-highlight that does a great job of highlighting words on any website page.

Here's an overview of the tool:
- Search and highlight multiple words on web pages.
- Highlight multiple English words on all pages.
- All your keywords will be saved.

Once you download the tool in Google Chrome, click on the "M" icon and add your search criteria. I would not recommend doing a full Boolean string but rather focus on individual keywords that you want to find on a page. Make sure to include each term within the bar and add a space between each.

For example:
Java spring agile
If you have hundreds of tabs open in your browser, this tool will become extremely helpful for you. It saves me around 30-60 seconds of my time per page while I scroll through to find the right keywords.

Honestly, this tool alone could help save you 20-30 minutes of your day. You could use that extra time to focus on the outreach and engagement pieces.

> A surprisingly large fraction of applicants, **even** those with masters' degrees and PhDs in computer science, fail during interviews when asked to carry out basic programming tasks. For example, I've personally interviewed graduates who can't answer "Write a loop that counts from 1 to 10" or "What's the number after F in hexadecimal?" Less trivially, I've interviewed many candidates who can't use recursion to solve a real problem. These are basic skills; anyone who lacks them probably hasn't done much programming.
>
> Speaking on behalf of software engineers who have to interview prospective new hires, I can safely say that we're tired of talking to candidates who can't program their way out of a paper bag. If you can successfully write a loop that goes from 1 to 10 in every language on your resume, can do simple arithmetic without a calculator, and can use recursion to solve a real problem, you're already ahead of the pack!

OneTab
Rating: Beginner
Features:
- Manage all your bookmark tabs in one place

Whenever you find yourself with too many tabs, click the OneTab icon to convert all your tabs into a list. When you need to access the tabs again, you can either restore them individually or all at once.

When your tabs are in the OneTab list, you will save memory and CPU utilization because you will have reduced the number of tabs open in your browser.

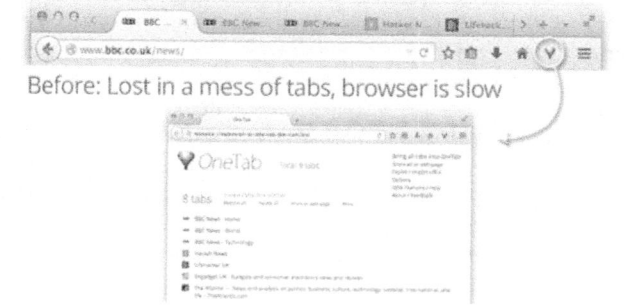

Recruiter Wand

Rating: Beginner
Features:
- Free extension
- Auto populate templates from LinkedIn profiles
- Sourcing and messaging capabilities

WizardSourcer has created a browser extension called Recruiter Wand. This free extension will allow the user to create auto-filled emails for contacts on LinkedIn or other social media platforms.

The extension will capture the names, company, and skills on the page and auto fill them into a template. The user can choose from a list of pre-saved templates. You can add additional templates within the tool as well. The user can then copy the auto-generated text and paste it into emails and other messaging platforms.

This tool was created out of frustration into filling in email templates for my recruiting messages. Why hasn't someone created a simple way to auto fill in recruiter templates with a lead's updated information?

What are the benefits to using this tool?
1. It's a free way to manage recruiter templates all in one place.
2. Select from a large variety of auto filled templates in many different industries.
3. Add and save additional recruiter templates within the tool.
4. Auto fill in templates with the applicant's most updated information.
5. Speed up you're sourcing and messaging abilities.
6. It's simple and easy to understand and use.

How to use this extension tool?
1. Download the extension in the Google Chrome store.
2. Search on LinkedIn or on a website page with resume details.
3. Select the Recruiter Wand tool to load in the Chrome browser.

4. Then go to a candidates LinkedIn profile select (Get LinkedIn Data) and auto fill in the template.
5. Include date of availability – easily give your availability for that day or week.
6. Once you've auto filled in the template select copy and then paste it into an email or InMail.

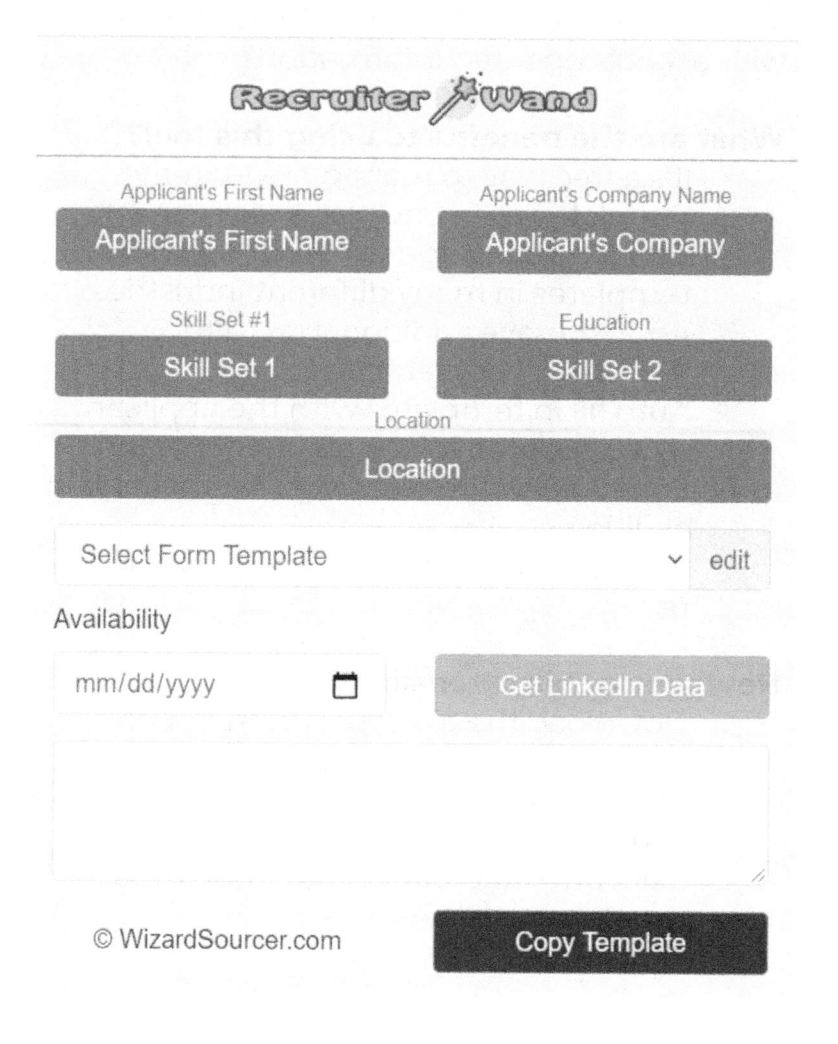

Recruiter Wand

Applicant's First Name	Applicant's Company Name
Applicant's First Name	Applicant's Company

Skill Set #1	Education
Skill Set 1	Skill Set 2

Location

Location

Select Form Template ⌄ | edit

Availability

mm/dd/yyyy | Get LinkedIn Data

© WizardSourcer.com | Copy Template

TextExpander

Rating: Intermediate
Features:
- Auto populates templates
- Save hundreds of templates all within one place
- Works on most website pages

TextExpander is an app that lets you summon up content with a couple of keystrokes.

Never type out or copy-paste the answer to a common prospect question again. Simply type a short abbreviation and watch it instantly expand into a text snippet with a full response. Best of all, it works anywhere you type so you can speak with candidates in their preferred channel.

Fill-in snippets are like "saved replies," but customizable. They can come with fill-in-the-blank form field or as a pop-up menu for choosing from a list of content options, like in the image below:

Personal details snippets include:
- Your first name (unless you have a two-letter name, that is)
- Last name
- Full name
- Email address
- Home addresses
- Personal website or blog URL

TextExpander helps you communicate quickly and effortlessly: you can write a complete email in seconds with just a couple of keystrokes.

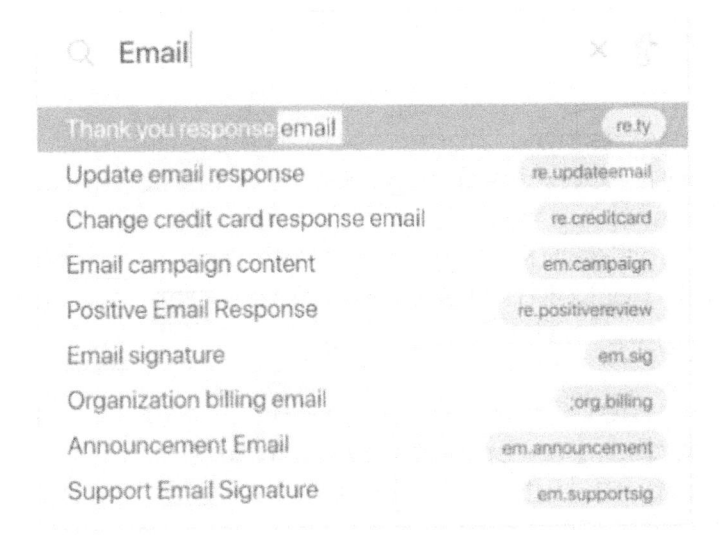

Thank you response email	re.ty
Update email response	re.updateemail
Change credit card response email	re.creditcard
Email campaign content	em.campaign
Positive Email Response	re.positivereview
Email signature	em.sig
Organization billing email	;org.billing
Announcement Email	em.announcement
Support Email Signature	em.supportsig

Save time
Even if your job doesn't require you to send speedy replies, typing shorthand will save you tons of time. You can save 30+ hours a month with TextExpander.

Prices range from $40 to $129 per year depending on the packages.

ChatGPT
Rating: Intermediate
Features:
- AI tool that can automate searches
- Create Boolean strings

- Optimize job descriptions
- Suggest recruiter messages

For years now there has been a prediction about how AI is going to take over recruiting. So far there have been some tools that have helped recruiters be more efficient and better, but most of the tools out there so far have not lived up to the hype.

In comes, Open AI's Chat GPT-3 which I know is not going to replace any recruiters at the moment, but it's the best AI tool that has been released to the public…

ChatGPT, as a language model, can potentially improve recruiting and talent sourcing in several ways:

Resume screening: ChatGPT can be trained on resumes to assist in the screening process by identifying keywords, qualifications, and experience that match the job requirements. This can help recruiters to quickly identify the most qualified candidates.

Writing job descriptions: ChatGPT can be used to generate clear and compelling job descriptions based on the job requirements and the company's culture, which can attract more diverse and qualified candidates.

Email and other communications: ChatGPT can be used to generate personalized and professional email and other communications with candidates, such as interview confirmation, rejection and offer letters. This can improve the candidate experience and increase engagement with the company.

Interview Assistance: ChatGPT can be used to generate interview questions based on the job requirements and the candidate's resume, helping recruiters to conduct more effective interviews.

Improving communication with candidates: ChatGPT can be used to create a chatbot that can interact with candidates, answering questions and providing information about the company and job openings. This can improve the candidate experience and increase engagement with the company.

It's important to note that ChatGPT is a language model, and it will output based on the input it has been trained on. Therefore, it's important to train it on diverse and inclusive data and set up the parameters accordingly. Additionally, it's important to have human oversight and review the output generated by ChatGPT, to ensure that it aligns with the company's recruitment policies and diversity and inclusion goals.

Could Chat GPT replace recruiters some day?
Recruiting is a complex process that involves many different tasks such as sourcing, assessing, and hiring candidates, as well as building relationships with potential candidates. These tasks require human skills such as communication, negotiation, and emotional intelligence.

Additionally, the recruitment process is also subject to legal and ethical considerations, which require human oversight and decision-making. ChatGPT can assist with these tasks, but it cannot replace the human aspect of recruiting, which involves the ability to understand, empathize, and connect with candidates.

Moreover, it's important to note that ChatGPT is a language model and it will output based on the input it has been trained on, it can also reflect bias and stereotypes if the data it has been trained on is not diverse and inclusive. Therefore, it is important to have human oversight and review the output generated by ChatGPT to ensure that it aligns with the company's recruitment policies and diversity and inclusion goals.

In conclusion, while ChatGPT can assist recruiters with certain tasks, it is unlikely that it will replace recruiters completely. Recruiting is a complex process that requires human skills and oversight.

Future prediction of recruiters with this type of tool?

Increased use of technology: As technology continues to advance, recruiters will use more automation and AI tools to streamline recruiting processes, such as resume screening and scheduling interviews. This will free up recruiters' time to focus on more strategic and value-added tasks such as building relationships with candidates and developing recruitment strategies.

I asked the tool: Write me a message to recruit a software engineer? Here's it's response:

Dear [Candidate],

We are currently looking for an experienced and talented software engineer to join our team at [Company Name]. We are excited to find someone who is passionate about technology and has a strong track record of developing high-quality software.

We are looking for someone who has experience in [specific programming languages, frameworks, etc.] and who is comfortable working in an Agile development environment. The ideal candidate will also have experience with [specific technologies, platforms, etc.] and a strong understanding of software development best practices.

As a software engineer at [Company Name], you will have the opportunity to work on exciting projects and to have a direct impact on the success of our company. We offer a competitive salary, flexible working hours, and a comprehensive benefits package.

If this opportunity interests you, please send your resume and a cover letter to [email/link]. We would love to hear from you and to learn more about your qualifications and experience.

We look forward to hearing from you!
Best regards, [Your Name] Recruiting Manager at [Company Name]

This tool will forever change the recruiting industry. I'm in shock and awe of its future uses and capabilities.

Conclusion

I hope you've gained insights crafting messages and have found value from these chapters. I'll admit, this book was very challenging to write. It took me over two years to demo and review over 50+ tools.

I've written on several topics within recruiting and have received so many kind notes and messages from recruiters across the world. I can't thank you enough for that. It has enlightened and humbled me greatly.

I would appreciate it if you would take the time to write an honest review about the book on Amazon so that others can also benefit from this publication.

Please follow WizardSourcer.com for my latest updates.